JAMES HOLLAND

THE FORGOTTEN ARTIST

by

Steve Bond

Published by
CHURNET VALLEY BOOKS
43 Bath Street, Leek, Staffordshire. 01538 399033

© Steve Bond and Churnet Valley Books 1999
ISBN 1 897949 49 9

Printed in Malta by Interprint Limited

To
Christine

Cover: Ospedale Civile, Venice 1858
Victoria and Albert Museum

CONTENTS

Appendices

ACKNOWLEDGEMENTS

This book could not have been written without the help of the following kind people and organisations who have willingly contributed time and effort in various ways to help with our researches over the last several years. My thanks to you all and to anyone I may have missed.

Gabrielle Norton of Thos Agnew & Sons Ltd, Bill Thompson of the Albany Gallery, Ashmolean Museum Oxford, Sarah Dodgson of The Athenaeum Club, Birmingham Museum and Art Gallery, Julie Moffat of Boston Museum of Fine Arts, Bristol City Art Gallery, The British Museum, Jeremy Parks of Christies, The Courtaulds Institute, Jane Wallis of Derby Museum and Art Gallery, Bernard Elsden the great grandson of Charles William Hird, Dr Louisa Connor of Eton College, Ferens Art Gallery Hull, Melissa Dalziel and Jane Munro of The Fitzwilliam Museum Cambridge, David Alston and Anne Goodchild of The Graves Art Gallery Sheffield, The Greater London Record Office, Julian Watson of Greenwich Art Gallery and Museum, Steven Whittles of The Harris Gallery Preston, Harrow School, Ann Sandford of Hereford Art Gallery and Museum, Andrea George of The Cecil Higgins Gallery Bedford, The Friends of Highgate Cemetery, Malcolm Holmes of Holborn Library, The Royal Holloway College Egham, Jacqueline Dugas of the Henry E. Huntington Library and Art Gallery San Marino California, Michael Ingram Esq, The Lady Lever Gallery Port Sunlight Liverpool, The Laing Gallery Newcastle, C.White of The Law Society, Leeds City Art Gallery, Miss Farr of Leicester City Museum, Lisbon City Museum, Manchester City Gallery, The Mellon Centre for Studies in British Art, Eric Vanasse of Montreal Museum of Fine Arts, Mireille Galinou of The Museum of London, Jill Trevelyan of The National Art Gallery Wellington, New Zealand, Richard Hemphill of The National Gallery of Canada Ottawa, David Taylor of The National Maritime Museum Greenwich, Dr Mark Evans of the National Museum of Wales Cardiff, John Chesshyre of The National Trust at Scotney Castle Kent, Chris Cove-Smith and Mr Gillett of National Westminster Bank, the late lamented Royal Naval College Greenwich, Roger Cooksey of the Newport Museum and Art Gallery, Neil Walker of the Nottingham Castle Museum, Messrs Phillips, Constance-Anne Parker of The Royal Academy of Arts, Charmian Highstead of The Royal Society of Painters in Water-Colours, Constance Thomson of The Ruskin Gallery Stratford-on-Avon, Henry Wemyss of Sotheby's, Margo Heller of Southampton City Art Gallery, Spink and Son Ltd, Barbara Roth of the Swiss Department of the Interior Geneva, Heidi Reisz of the Swiss National Tourist Office London, Jackie Riding of The Tate Gallery, the late Morley Tonkin, The Victoria and Albert Museum, Mr Vella of Wakefield Art Gallery, The Walker Art Gallery Liverpool, Terry McGowan of the Art Gallery of Western Australia Perth, The Whitworth Gallery Manchester, Deborah Dean of Worcester Art Gallery, and especially Mary Griffiths, Sarah MacDonald, Jennifer Rennie and all the other wonderful people at the Stoke City Art Gallery, my sister Janet Rose who has also spent many hours pouring through remote and dusty archives, my cousins Ted and Jocelyn Milligan who have been of invaluable help with the North American and Portugese research, and last but my no means least my wife Christine who has shared the enthusiasm, encouraged and cajoled when it was needed and seen this lengthy project through with me.

INTRODUCTION
JAMES HOLLAND 1799-1870
The Forgotten Artist

Amongst the elegant decay of the Victorian Valhalla that is the great cemetery at Highgate in North London, lie the mortal remains of 170,000 souls including many who achieved fame, fortune or simply notoriety during their lifetime.

There are magnificent mausolea erected at vast expense by the powerful families of Victorian society, and many a tourist is today eagerly guided to gaze upon the last resting place of the Beers, Dickens, Nelsons, Faradays and their contemporaries. Yet, in a still neglected part of the jungle that Highgate has become, and away from the regular paths along which the curious are lead, there reposes, under a simple headstone, the body of one of the era's greatest water-colourists, whose works are still avidly collected by art lovers around the globe, but who is sadly neglected as a man of his time.

Highgate, a late eighteenth century photograph from *The Queen's London* .

James Holland does not even appear on the cemetery's list of notables, and yet this talented, family-loving man from Staffordshire had taken London by the throat and with others of like mind, had helped to shake the early 19th century art world out of its romantic complacency and into the realms of brilliant colour and reality.

On the 13th day of February 1870, mid-Victorian England was caught in the grip of a severe spell of stormy late winter weather. The national daily newspapers were reporting many deaths from starvation amongst the poorer sections of English society, and continually appealing for funds to aid the ever increasing numbers of orphaned children being taken into the care of the various charitable institutions. There was a major colliery disaster to add to the misery of the populace and in London, the police were investigating a dreadful murder that had taken place the previous day on Waterloo Bridge.

Far removed from all this turmoil, in an elegant four-storey Regency house at number eight Osnaburgh Street, not far from Regent's Park, an affluent and well-respected gentleman in the seventy-first year of his eventful life had finally breathed his last. James Holland, who had been attended anxiously by both his devoted lover and her sister, who was also his housekeeper, failed to awaken from his night's sleep. An urgent message was sent to his long-time friend and physician, Dr Charles Chinner Fuller, who was summoned that Friday morning, through the bitter wind and driving rain, from his practice in nearby Albany Street, but there was nothing he could do. Cirrhosis of the liver and exhaustion, he declared, had taken their final and inevitable toll.

It had been half a century earlier that the young James Holland had turned away from his childhood home in Burslem, the pottery town close to Stoke-on-Trent, to seek his fortune as an artist amongst the bright lights of

A contemporary engraving of London

the then far-distant capital. His mother's talent for painting had rubbed off on her son and had lead to his serving an apprenticeship in the John Davenport pottery works in Stoke-on-Trent; his early still-life water-colours are an echo of this period. However, he yearned to break free from the restrictions of endless flower, fruit and bird painting on china tea services and journeyed to London - a bold adventure for such a young man - but one which would prove to be the making of him. Living at first in Greenwich, he later established himself and his by then complex family, in the parish of St. Pancras, where he spent most of the rest of his life.

His astonishing talent for vibrant colour and atmosphere, especially when painting in his favourite medium water-colour, was to lead to much praise from his perhaps more distinguished, and certainly better known contemporaries. Swiftly progressing to move amongst the highest levels of Victorian society where he was much in demand as a tutor, it is believed he gave painting lessons to Queen Victoria, possibly during visits to Knole House in Kent, where they were both regular guests.. Holland travelled extensively on the Continent and his many studies of France, The Netherlands, Switzerland, and especially Portugal and Venice, are widely regarded as being among his finest works. His passion for painting is reflected in the extraordinary number of works he is known to have produced - there was a huge collection in his studio at the time of his death. He once remarked; *"Parting with a sketch was like parting with a tooth, once sold it cannot be replaced."*

Royal Academy from *The Graphic* 1880

Although he was elected to both the Water-colour Society (later Royal) and the Society of British Artists, it is strange that Holland never received the recognition he so richly deserved from the Royal Academy of Arts, where he was nevertheless a regular exhibitor. This curious oversight by the art establishment of the time has its legacy even today, where his important contribution to British art is all too often overlooked in studies of the Victorian era. A contemporary of Holland remarked in an article in 1843 when some will argue, his skill was at its height: *"I have seen....works by James Holland which were I think, as near perfection as water-colour can be carried - for bona fide truth, refined and finished to the highest degree."* (Modern Painters, Ruskin).

In 1949, The Leger Galleries in London's Old Bond Street, held one of the very few major exhibitions of Holland's work and an introduction to the catalogue was written by Martin Hardie CBE, Hon. RWS, a former keeper of the Department of Paintings at the Victoria and Albert Museum. He described the exhibition works as portraying *"Holland at his best and lifting him into the highest ranks of our water-colour school."* Hardie goes on to say;

"Holland, like others of the Contemporary group with whom he is associated (Bonington, Boys, Callow, Harding, David Roberts among them) was first and foremost a draughtsman. He uses a line that is sure, swift, legible and admirably constructive. Many drawings show how he could work in a shorthand rapidity of nervous impulsive strokes, and yet concentrate on delicacy and precision when they were required. Bonington died in 1828, winning wide reputation during Holland's most impressionable period, and from that great master of the lively outdoor sketch Holland undoubtedly learned much."

"This exhibition includes a series of sketches made in Portugal, Venice, Delft, Rotterdam and Genoa. In all of these, Holland's searching and vigorous pencil

John Constable

Joshua Reynolds

Joseph Mallord William Turner

Richard Parkes Bonnington

Dante Gabriel Rosetti

John Ruskin

William Morris

John Everett Millais

Some contemporaries of James Holland

work is combined with a tactful and restrained use of colour washes, which give delightfully the suggestion rather than the full reality of the colour scheme before his eyes; only here and there does he place gay and enlivening notes of local colour. Of special interest are a few purely atmospheric studies of sky and weather, to which, like Constable, he adds notes of the time of day and the movement of the clouds - an unexpected unfamiliar Holland this. In all the sketches made in Portugal and Italy, the artist's hand seems to have hovered over the paper, dropping a touch of joyous colour here and there till the whole scene is animated, fluttering, enveloped in light. The James Holland of this mood still awaits the enhanced reputation which this exhibition should help to justify."

The Dictionary of National Biography similarly assessed him as *"One of the finest colourists of the English School"*. Henry Wemyss of Sotheby's British Paintings and Water-colours Department said in 1995 that James Holland *"had original talent and although his fine early works owe something to Bonington, after the mid 1830s he developed a style of painting in both water-colour and oil which is extremely sophisticated and very much his own. He has been rather badly treated by writers and exhibition organisers in the past and consequently the (auction) value of his work is in most cases surprisingly low."*

In addition to the 30 Hollands hung during his lifetime by the Royal Academy, the British Institution showed 91, the Society of British Artists 106 and the Water-colour Society well in excess of 200. He received an Honourable Mention at the Paris International Exhibition of 1855, and was further honoured by two loan exhibitions; the Manchester Art Treasures in 1857 and the International Exhibition in 1862.

More than a century and a quarter since his death, the hundreds of surviving works of this prolific and much-travelled artist are the prized possessions of many collectors both public and private. Virtually all the major and provincial galleries in the United Kingdom, plus many of the major national collections overseas, boast Hollands in their collections, the largest selections being in the Victoria and Albert Museum which has 45 works and the Stoke City Art Gallery with 40. Regrettably it is all too rare to find any of these works actually hanging on the walls. Others regularly appear in the big London auction houses and sell for sums that would have astounded the artist even in his comfortable circumstances of long ago.

Although Holland's talent is well appreciated and respected by both the art world and the many private collectors who seek his work, the details of his extraordinary private life have until now been a closed book. There have been attempts in the past to document his life, most notably by the late Morley Tonkin of Powysland Newspapers who published a short piece in the late 1960s, which despite being an excellent starting point, posed as many questions as it answered. Subsequently, extensive research over many years by Holland's descendants through long forgotten records in various national archives and family papers, have revealed an intriguing story which affords a fascinating insight into the life and times of a Victorian gentleman.. The result is this first ever close look at a man who has been rightly described as one of the leading landscape artists of his day.

The Family Tree of Martha Holland

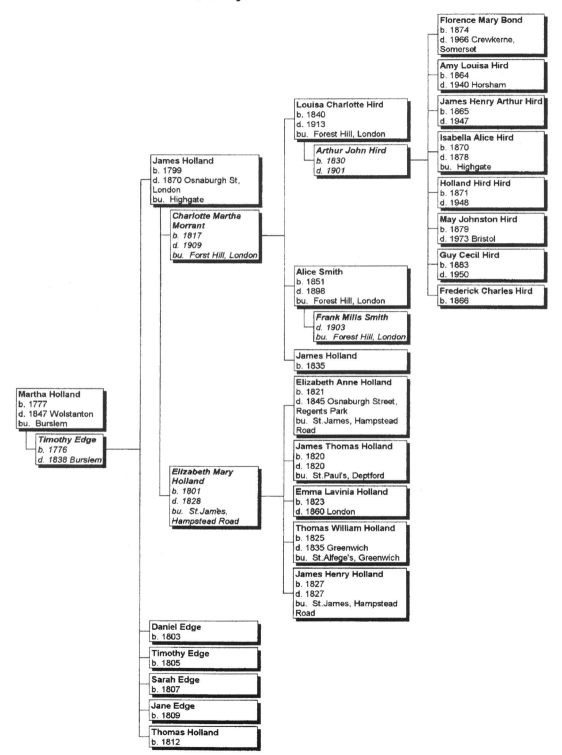

CHAPTER ONE
A BURSLEM LAD

In the county of Staffordshire in the English North Midlands is the sprawling town of Stoke-on-Trent, which came into being in its present form in 1910 by combining the old town of the same name with the five adjoining towns of Burslem, Fenton, Hanley, Longton and Tunstall. For centuries the whole area had been known as The Potteries, indeed the Romans are known to made pottery here, and the great names in British pottery - Coalport, Minton, Spode, Wedgwood - all established themselves in and around the five towns during the eighteenth century. The area was particularly suited to this trade thanks to ready supplies of both cheap local coal for the pottery kilns and good quality clay for the production of the earthenware boxes, or saggers, used to protect fine wares during the firing process. From the eighteenth century, there was also access to a burgeoning canal network, both to bring in the soapstone and china clay from the West Country, and to transport the finished wares to the customers. As for Burslem itself, so important in this story, it was Josiah Wedgwood's birthplace in 1730 and the Wedgwood Memorial Institute today stands on the site of his first factory.

The Red Lion Inn Burslem, near the Market Place, in the early 19th century.

The family name Holland has always been fairly common in the Midlands, largely descendants of early Dukes and Earls and one Thomas Holland, born in 1748, became a notable potter in the Derby china works, and is said to have been responsible for introducing the shiny black and red china-ware which was much in vogue in America in the latter part of that century. On 9 September 1769 he married a Jemima Cartledge in Stoke. She was herself a painter of flowers on pottery and porcelain, but as was so typical in those times was illiterate and the marriage register shows that she simply entered her mark.

Thomas and Jemima went to live in Burslem, where he had set up his own works, and their son Isaac was born on 19 August 1770. The first of so many tragedies which were to strike the Holland family came however, just four months later with the death of Jemima, nine days before Christmas. Then on 31 March 1772 the burial of the infant Isaac was recorded, a bitter and total end to Thomas's first marriage. Three years after the death of his wife however, on 26 January 1773, he was back in Stoke and marrying again. His bride this time was Tomason Allen -

again illiterate judging by the register - and Thomas taught her flower painting so that she could work alongside him in what had become quite a family business at the Hill Top works, with various brothers and nephews coming and going over the next few years. The works were in what used to be called Liverpool Road, Burslem and was later renamed Westport Road. Modern industrial premises now cover the site.

The couple lived at The Green Head, Burslem and had six children altogether, although three of them died in infancy - an all too common occurrence in the Potteries. Their third child was a daughter, Martha (preceded by two others of the same name who failed to survive), who at the age of twenty two gave birth on Wednesday 16 October 1799 to an illegitimate son whom she named James Holland - the artist to be. An often repeated error in art reference books gives James's year of birth as 1800, but the Burslem parish register is quite clear that it was actually a year earlier. However, that same register disagrees on the exact date with the artist's headstone in Highgate cemetery, which says 17 October.

Thomas and Tomason lived on until July 1807 and November 1805 respectively, and were buried in the same grave in the south-west corner of Burslem churchyard. Regrettably after many years of neglect and vandalism, the churchyard was largely cleared of headstones at some stage during the 1980s, and the Holland's was one of those to be removed.

James Holland was born in 1799. About a year after James's birth, Martha married one Timothy Edge, who was then about 24 years old (b.1776) and was variously described as being both a farmer and a maker of fine china figures and ornaments - or "toys" as they were then called. He worked in Thomas Holland's pottery at Hill Top and shared a farm with him between Burslem and Wolstanton, called Barnfield. Following the death of Thomas Holland, his estate was divided such that his son Thomas and Timothy Edge shared the Hill Top works and the farm between them. This situation continued until Thomas's death, when his wife Ann took over the works completely, and in return Timothy acquired her share of the farm.

A typical Burslem view in the early 1800s.

There is no way of knowing for sure whether Timothy Edge was James's natural father, but it seems to have been a stable family environment and it was at the farm that James was brought up until at least 1812. During this period it is

Two other famous sons of Burslem. Josiah Wedgwood died four years before James Holland's birth. Arnold Bennett was born there three years before his death.

Views of Burslem in the first half of the 18th century which would be familiar to James Holland: Enoch Wood's pottery works above and the Town Hall below.

clear that the family tradition of painting must have been aroused in the child, and he no doubt would have received tuition from his mother and possibly even his grandmother. In fact Henry Ottley in his book *Biographical and Critical Dictionary of Recent and Living Artists* which was published in 1866, records that it had indeed been Tomason who had taught him to paint, although as she died when he was still very young, the main influence is more likely to have been his mother.

During these formative years Martha and Timothy had five more children; Daniel in 1803, Timothy 1805, Sarah 1807, Jane 1809 and Thomas in 1812 who would also ultimately become an artist. Daniel and Timothy were to go into partnership as makers of fine china figures.

On Christmas Day in 1805, Martha and Timothy took James who was by then six years old, together with two year old Daniel and the newborn Timothy, to Burslem church to be baptised. In his researches, Morley Tonkin speculated over the reason for this multiple baptism, and considered it most likely to have been either a result of pressure from the local clergy, or more simply the dying wish of Tomason who had passed away six weeks earlier. There is a possible clue in the register recording this event, that Timothy was not James's father. The child was entered as *"son of Martha Holland, illegt"*

Burslem church, engraving around 1830.

and as the couple were by that time married, the more usual entry *"son of Martha Holland and Timothy Edge"* might have been expected if the latter wished to pronounce James as being his own offspring.

At the age of twelve it was time for James to go to work. As the Holland business was quite small and many of the family already worked there, it was decided to apprentice him elsewhere and he was taken on by John Davenport at Longport Hall which would probably have meant him leaving the farm to lodge with relatives nearer the works. Davenport had established himself at Longport in 1794 and by the turn of the century had taken over a number of other failed potteries along the Staffordshire canal, including those of John Brindley (whose premises were those first occupied by Davenport), Edward Bourne, Walter Daniel and Robert Williamson, building a substantial fortune as a result. One of Davenport's trainees was a Cornish seaman's son by the name of Joshua Cristell, who later became one of the founders of the Water Colour Society with which James would have so many connections. The pottery was successful in many ways, finding favour with the highest in the land by Royal Appointment to King William IV not long after James's apprenticeship had finished, before finally closing down in 1887.

Holland's own notes (which regrettably have disappeared in the last twenty five years or so), apparently recorded that he took two sample paintings along to Davenport's, one of flowers and the other of a linnet, and was taken on as an apprentice there and then, to learn the art

Longport Hall. The home of W. Davenport.

of painting flowers, fruit and birds on china. He would probably have found much of his time there enjoyable, since the work was more varied than in many of the potteries and Davenport had a reputation for being well up with the trends and fashions of the day.

He completed his seven year apprenticeship in the spring of 1819 and then had to decide what to do with himself. Although a talented young artist could easily find plenty of work in the area, life in the five towns was grim. The air was constantly smoke-laden from the hundreds of kilns and furnaces which burned day and night. Dozens of potteries operated as small family-run affairs, with whole hosts of relatives including many small children labouring away for long hours in extremely arduous conditions. Indeed many of the materials used for colouring and

Pottery made around 1820 at Davenports.

glazing pottery were extremely hazardous to health, and the entries in the Burslem burial registers bear stark testimony to just how perilous life there could be.

The family business was being run by James's aunt Ann while Timothy and Daniel Edge had started their own business the year before, with three sons who could ultimately succeed Timothy if all went well. Doubtless too, James was well aware, if only from talk in the Davenport works, of Joshua Cristell who had successfully escaped the potteries to found the Water Colour Society in London. The Capital then as now, seemed to offer the promise of a brighter future and James decided to take the plunge.

At this point James's own sense of humour and penchant for leg-pulling or even downright fibbing, intrudes on official versions of his life for the first time. He obviously enjoyed a laugh at the expense of the establishment, and nowhere is that more evident than in the inaccuracies in various previous attempts to recount his early days away from the Potteries.

The Dictionary of National Biography states that *"he came to London in 1819 to practice as a flower painter and to give lessons in drawing landscapes, architecture and marine subjects."* This is quite clearly wrong, for the twenty year old had spent his formative years painting predominantly flowers, fruit and birds on pottery, and had in all probability never even seen the sea. It would in fact be nine years before he exhibited his first landscape, twelve for his first architectural subject and thirteen for his first seascape, so it is highly likely that this information came from the artist himself either as deliberate mischief or simply as vague responses which were then misinterpreted.

There is no disputing the fact that he did not immediately settle in London, which would have been beyond the reach of his limited means at that time in any case. For a budding painter this was a blow, since the established artists were centred around St.Pancras and Marylebone and of course, the artists suppliers and art dealers were all in the city centre. He went instead to Deptford, which was then a small town of less than 20,000 inhabitants, well beyond the outer reaches of the suburbs in lovely unspoilt countryside. Travelling into London meant a lengthy coach ride, as the railway which was still really in its infancy, would not reach here for another seventeen years. So why come here? Other than cost, it is likely that he was attracted by the opportunity to sustain himself by working in one of the five potteries in Deptford at that time in order to finance his longer term artistic ambitions, which he may have helped to fuel by taking landscape lessons from James Webb who was then giving tuition in the area. The potential employers were the Perry family and Hopkins & Northern in Copperas Lane (later Bronze Street), Thomas Callaway Keeling on Tanner's Hill, plus George Marshall and Samuel Waylett in Church Street. James found a position in the Perry family business and seemed to land on his feet, for within a year of arriving in Deptford he had courted and married a local girl.

CHAPTER TWO

A FAMILY MAN

Elizabeth Mary Evans was married to James Holland on Monday 24 January 1820 at St.Paul's parish church Deptford, the third publication of their banns having been made at the evening service of the same church the previous day. She was a local girl, described as being *"of full age"* (she was baptised on 13 November 1799), and had a twin sister called Hanna, of whom nothing more is known. Her father William was a labourer and her mother's name was Mary; the family home was in Furnleys Lane. None of the parents signed the register, although the rector Thomas William McGuire noted that the marriage took place with the consent of Holland's parents since he was still a minor. The ceremony was witnessed by Sarah Morgan and Reuben Cox, a sexton, stone-mason and undertaker who frequently signed the register.

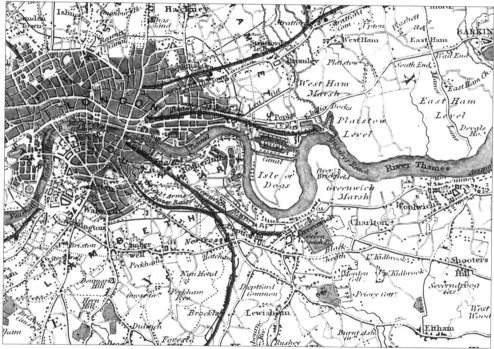

The London of James Holland, published in 1830 (James Moule).

Just two months later on 30 March, Elizabeth gave birth to a boy, whom they named James Thomas; in the birth register the father is described as being a *"painter in enamels."* At about the same time, James and Elizabeth moved to 33 Townsend Street, just off the Old Kent Road in Southwark, which was in the London suburbs and thus that much closer to the art world he yearned to break into. The house no longer survives, the site having been redeveloped some years ago for council flats. James was described as the householder in the Southwark rate-books, so presumably he was still working regularly, and on 23 April their son was baptised at St. Paul's, again by Thomas William McGuire. It seems they had already moved again, this time to Queen Street, but the baby was probably already not a well child, as on 13 May 1820 the couple went back yet again to St. Paul's church to bury him at the tender age of six weeks. This time William McGuire recorded the father's occupation as "gentleman".

BURIALS in the Parish of _St Paul Deptford_ in the County of _Kent_ in the Year 18_20_				
Name.	Abode.	When buried.	Age.	By whom the Ceremony was performed.
Bragger Mary ann Daug.r of Alex.r & Eliz.th No. 369.	Grove Street Blockmaker	May 12th	months 10	Tho.s Wilson McGuire Rector
Holland Ja.s Thomas son of Ja.s & Eliz.th No. 370.	Queen Street Clerk	May 13th	weeks 6	Tho.s Wilson McGuire Rector
au...	Flaggon Row	May...	...	Tho.s Wilson...

There was now a quiet period for James and Elizabeth, during which he would have been continuing his efforts to establish himself as an artist. In Roget's History of the Old Water Colour Society the author records from Holland himself that he sold his first twelve water-colours, all of flowers, for a total of ten shillings, but it is not clear exactly when this was. Inspired by this success, he then increased his price to five shillings each and the dealer Ackermann was one of his early customers. Meanwhile, on 25 September 1821 Elizabeth gave birth to their first daughter, Elizabeth Ann, who was baptised the following month at the church of St.George the Martyr. There can be little doubt then, that the two loved each other and had not simply been forced into an unwanted marriage by the imminent arrival of their first born child.

Once again there was little obvious artistic activity for a while, but by 1823 the family was living in Marylebone, no doubt in pursuit of James's continued desire to get closer to the established artists territory. The exact date of his move across the river was not recorded, but his second daughter Emma Lavinia was born on 27 August 1823 and registered in the St. Marylebone parish - the parish church being the scene of her baptism a few weeks later. James may have continued to receive painting tuition in Marylebone, but his financial circumstances would have precluded him from being a full-time pupil and all the available evidence points to his being largely self-taught. In fact the earliest known surviving work to be signed and dated by James was a water-colour of flowers completed in 1820, and now in the collection of the Fitzwilliam Museum in Cambridge.

James sketched by his friend John Scarlett Davis in 1824.

He did make acquaintance with fellow artists, notably with William Henry ("Bird's Nest") Hunt, the noted pastoral artist, who painted Holland in his studio in 1828; this fine water-colour study of the dashing young artist is now in the Victoria and Albert museum collection. Their firm friendship lasted right up until Hunt's death in 1864 and Holland often practised figures and portraiture using Hunt's daughter as a model. However, he never quite got to grips with painting people, especially in close-up, and they tended to be incidental to the main subject in nearly all his work. Despite his discomfort with the human form, he nevertheless established a trade mark by which so many of his works can still be instantly recognised, a figure dressed partially in red, usually in the middle distance.

The year after Emma was born, the Hollands moved yet again, this time to 23 Warren Street off Tottenham Court Road in the parish of St.Pancras. In those days this was a popular street with artists, mainly consisting of early Georgian terraces. James was apparently still simply renting part of a house, since he does not appear in the St.Pancras rate-books of the time. The street later declined significantly, with many of the ground floors being converted into small shops. Nevertheless, today 23 Warren Street is one of the few of Holland's many identified London addresses where the building survives in a recognisable original form. It was whilst living here that James's first major breakthrough into the art establishment occurred, for in April 1824 he was informed that one of his works *A Group of Flowers*, had been accepted for that year's Royal Academy exhibition in Somerset House, news which must have caused much rejoicing.

By April 1825 the Hollands were living at 51 London Street (now Maple Street) off Fitzroy Square, a site now covered by the Telecom tower complex, although some of the more

23 Warren Street (right) in the 1980s.

fortunate surrounding streets still retain the flavour of their nineteenth century appearance. On 1 June, their second son was born and baptised Thomas William three weeks later by the Reverend J Brackenbury at St. Pancras parish church; this time the father's profession was simply given as "artist". By an extraordinary coincidence, exactly two years to the day after Thomas was born, the couple's third son arrived. Once again the Reverend Brackenbury officiated when they had him baptised James Henry in September, the long delay being caused it is believed, by a family trip back to Burslem to show the children to their grandmother Martha Edge. Dated works painted in various parts of the north east of England lend support to this theory.

For many years the subsequent fates of these two sons were shrouded in mystery, with various theories being expounded, and the lengthy trail which finally uncovered the truth proved to be fascinating. Morley Tonkin stated in his notes that he could find no trace of either of them after their baptism and he speculated that there had been some matrimonial strife leading to separation, since he had also lost track of Elizabeth at about the same time. Death and burial records, such as they were in those days, had been searched without success, and there the matter rested until the late 1980s. At that time, Holland's present day descendants appealed through the genealogical press for contact with any other members of the family who might have been descended from either of the sons.

A very long shot though this was, it amazingly yielded a response from a family in Sussex who had an extraordinary tale to tell. Their belief was that at some time around 1829 or 1830, the relationship between James and Elizabeth had indeed been in crisis and that she had fallen for a worker in a London silk warehouse. The story went on to say that one day, while James had been out for a walk with his daughters, Elizabeth had run off with her lover taking the two young boys with her. For some reason, presumably to protect the boys, they then decided to keep the surname Holland and one of the sons - Thomas William - subsequently grew to adulthood and started a new family line leading to the Sussex descendants.

At first all the pieces appeared to fit and it seemed that at last the mystery of at least one of the sons had been solved. However, there were one or two nagging doubts, not least that in none of the photographs of the supposed Thomas William and subsequent generations, could any likeness with James or his known descendants be seen. Furthermore, it seemed rather unlikely that given the strong Victorian family values and attitudes which tended to favour male offspring, a proud father would choose to walk out with his daughters alone, leaving his sons at home. Then in 1994, while searching through some rather obscure burial records for another member of the family, the truth was unexpectedly unearthed.

The first discovery was that James Henry had only survived for six months, being buried at St.James Hampstead Road in December 1827. Immediately after this the burial record was found for Elizabeth, in the same cemetery five months later. Thus it was obviously not possible for them to have run off with another man a year or two later. The final piece which was necessary to be able to completely discount the Sussex theory, was found a week or two later in yet another little known archive. Thomas William had only lived to reach the age of ten years before being buried at St.Alfege's church in Greenwich (James had moved to the area some five years previously), and so the sad brief lives of all James's sons had been established. As for the Sussex connection, it would appear that their Thomas William Holland, presumably unsure of his own birth date, needed to obtain a copy of his birth certificate in order to claim a pension following an industrial injury while working in the Royal Mint, and on searching through the records of the day plumped for the first one he found in 1825 - the baptismal details for James's son.

(During the course of this research another Thomas William Holland was found to have been born in London later in that same year - presumably the Sussex family's true ancestor).

To return to London Street. Apart from all the family events, James was having further success with his painting. He was in the 1825 Royal Academy exhibition with *Flowers* and again a year later with *Flowers* and *Study of Belladonna Lily after Nature*. In 1827 he was back again with *Sketch of Wild Flowers - Composition*, and in that same year began a long association with the Society of British Artists (now the Royal Society of British Artists), when he exhibited a water-colour entitled *Study of Flowers after Nature*. It would appear that he sought consolation from the tragic loss of James Henry later that year by immersing himself in a frenzy of activity, for at the March 1828 selection for that year's Society of British Artists exhibition, no fewer than nine of his water-colours were chosen, five of flowers and four of fruit.

The family was also on the move again, perhaps they wished to escape all the unpleasant memories that London Street now held, or it could be that they were advised to leave the city centre for the cleaner air of the suburbs, for it is now clear that Elizabeth must have been far from well, probably ever since the birth of her last son. James may also have had in the back of his mind the idea that in the suburbs there were many private schools or academies as they were then styled, which might prove a useful source of income if he could give painting lessons, since the ability to draw and paint were considered part of the necessary social graces, especially for young ladies. Good tutors were in great demand, and Holland was young, presentable and a successful Royal Academy exhibitor. Whatever the actual reason was, early in April 1828 the Hollands moved to 4 Queen's Row Camberwell. A mere month later he returned to central London to bury his wife Elizabeth alongside James Henry in the Hampstead Road cemetery.

Camberwell was a green and pleasant outer London suburb in 1828, the area generally being the preserve of the well-to-do with large houses. Queen's Row was a Georgian terrace at the town end of Grove Lane, which commanded fine views across the still heavily wooded countryside and which must have set the young artist thinking about the future direction of his work. Thus far all his exhibited paintings had been of flowers or fruit and he wished to branch out into landscape work. This is evident from the close attention he paid to the work of Richard Parkes Bonington, who was three years Holland's junior, but who was making a great name for himself whilst living on the Continent through particularly vibrant use of water-colour in all his landscapes.

Bonington had returned to England briefly in both 1825 and 1827 and it is believed that he and Holland met on at least one of these occasions since, after Bonington's death within a few days of returning yet again in 1828, two water-colours by Holland were found among his possessions. The two works were *View on the Medway* and *Woody Dell* both painted in 1827. There can be little doubt that Bonington was a great influence on Holland; both the style of his work and his choice of Continental subjects between 1829 and about 1840 clearly demonstrate this.

In the meantime, his success at the Royal Academy continued, with three pictures being accepted in the summer of 1828, two were of flowers and the other was his first exhibited landscape **Liscard Mill Liverpool**, doubtless painted during the trip to see his mother the previous year. On only one other occasion, in 1850, would he get three paintings into one Royal Academy exhibition. By stark contrast, he failed to get in at all in 1829, although this disappointment was amply compensated by having seven works accepted for the Society of British Artists, of which three were oils - very probably his first in this medium to be shown. Also in 1829, Holland began exhibiting at the British Institution, and continued to do so up until two years before his death when the lease of their exhibition rooms expired. On this first occasion he had two oils on show - the British Institution having adopted a no water-colours policy by this time.

While his work was beginning to settle, his domestic life was certainly not, since before 1829 was out he would move twice more, first to 24 Rathbone Place Marylebone (just off Oxford Street), which survives with a largely unaltered period facade, and then just a few doors down the same street to number 14. The explanation for these moves in such quick succession may be either that the lure of the artists area of London was proving hard to resist, or more likely, these were actually only studio addresses to which he travelled from Camberwell. This latter theory seems to be supported by the fact that early the following year he had moved again in the same street, this time to number 51 which, by a great coincidence is now the site of an important artists materials shop! By April he had settled at 3 Union Place Greenwich which was one of a short row of terraced houses. (The houses were all derelict by the 1960s and demolished shortly thereafter, the site now being covered by modern industrial premises at number 54 Blackheath Road).

24 Rathbone Place in the 1980s.

This move was to herald one of the most significant periods in his life. He was to stay here for no less than fifteen years, during which time he commenced his Continental travels and reached what many believe to have been the height of his talent as an artist. Not only that, he was also to enter into a second, at times stormy, but ultimately long-lasting relationship.

CHAPTER THREE

THE TRAVELLING ARTIST

The Greenwich and Blackheath area inspired Holland to make his first sustained efforts in landscape work. Being some six miles down river from the heart of London, Blackheath was still a truly wild and beautiful place in 1830, dotted with meandering streams and water mills, while along the riverside at Greenwich there were any number of attractive and bustling boatyards. Dominating the south bank of the Thames was Christopher Wren's magnificent Royal Naval Hospital, later the Royal Naval College, which was built on the site of a fifteenth century royal palace as a refuge for sick and disabled seamen. Although Holland was to paint it a great many times, this new found inspiration was not reflected in his exhibition submissions that year, for his one acceptance at the Royal Academy was *Composition of Flowers,* while the British Institution showed *Study of Flowers*; both were oils.

Greenwich, King William's Quadrangle
James Holland, Watercolour. Private Collection.

In that same year he travelled abroad for the first time, since there are water-colours showing Paris scenes dated 1830, but unfortunately no further details of this trip are known. It is likely however, that this was only a short visit, since no other Continental works bearing that date have come to light; perhaps he was feeling his way on this first journey across the Channel and was reluctant to be away from his motherless children for too long a time. Travel across the Channel had been made considerably easier in 1825 with the introduction of steam packet services from both London and the Channel ports, operated by the General Steam Navigation Company. Holland also produced a lot of work during that same summer in and around both Greenwich and parts of Kent, including a water-colour *Beckenham Church Porch* which is now in the National Art Gallery in Wellington, New Zealand. All this effort was reflected in the completely changed nature of his exhibited work in 1831.

A House in Greenwich
James Holland,
Watercolour, 1839.
Huntington Library.

View on the Medway
James Holland,
Watercolour, 1830.
Private Collection.

*The Thames below
Woolwich*
James Holland,
Watercolour, 1843.
Tate Gallery.

Porch at Beckenham Church, Kent
James Holland, Watercolour, 1830. National Art Gallery Wellington N.Z.

The Royal Academy selected his first publicly displayed architectural work *College Gate, Rochester* and the Society of British Artists marked another breakthrough - his first of only a very small number of hung portraits. These were an oil and a water-colour both entitled *Greenwich Pensioner*, while the same gallery also chose water-colours of Greenwich Hospital and a village church. The Greenwich theme was continued at the British Institution with an oil of the hospital together with another version of the 1828 Liscard Mill work. During this time he also began the first of several studies of *View of London from Blackheath*, before setting off on his second visit to France in the autumn. He again went to Paris, this time in the company of his good friend John Scarlett Davis whom he had known since at least 1824, when John had sketched him working in his studio. Davis had a reputation for being something of a drunkard, but it is believed this was in fact undeserved. The trip resulted in James's first exhibited Continental subject, *Cathedral of St. Denis* which found its way into the Royal Academy in 1832.

That same year 1832, was the only one over a thirty-three year period in which he failed to get selected for the British Institution, but the Society of British Artists took another water-colour from the Paris trip, *Palace of Phillipe le Bel.* He went back to his roots for the remaining three works exhibited that spring, as they were all nature studies, one oil and two water-colours. Later in the year, the Society of British Artists which had up until then staged a single major exhibition each May to July when *"the tasteful and opulent are usually resident in the Metropolis"*, decided to make better use of its Suffolk Street galleries by also holding a winter exhibition. They decided to feature the work of both living and notable dead artists, and James had six pictures accepted, split equally between oils and water-colours. One of the oils and two of the water-colours were studies from nature, probably painted on Blackheath, while the remaining two oils were *Gateway* and

Southend Bridge, which was probably a bridge over one of the streams in Deptford or Greenwich. The third water-colour was ***London from Blackheath*** and, evidently, it attracted considerable attention; this important milestone work in Holland's development is believed to be that of the same scene now in the Harris Gallery in Preston.

He did not travel abroad again in either 1832 or for the following two years, consolidating his blossoming reputation as a landscape artist with more work in the area around his home. During late January he recorded the demolition work on the old 12th century London Bridge, which had been closed the previous year after being replaced by John Rennie's bridge begun in 1824, with a water-colour now in the

Paris Street Scene
James Holland, Watercolour, 1831. Private Collection.

Museum of London. He obviously still felt he should stay close to home at this time, as he had a young family to look after. Thomas William, his only surviving son, was seven years old now, and there were also the two girls, Elizabeth who was eleven and probably burdened with many of the household chores, and Emma who was nine. Since the death of James's wife Elizabeth some four years previously, there seems to have been no relationship in his life, so the pressures in his home life must have been intense, since although James was now beginning to do well as an artist, he doubtless could not yet afford much in the way of paid domestic help with the children. It is also conceivable that his late wife's relatives had rallied round after her death and were helping James to raise the children - another possible reason for reluctantly abandoning the artist's haunts of Marylebone to return south of the river.

His 1833 exhibiting season was successful if not in numbers, then at least with the standard of his work which drew much admiration. The Royal Academy took a single but impressive oil ***View of London from Blackheath***, the British Institution returning to the fold with the acceptance of ***Front View of Greenwich Hospital*** and the Society of British Artists took a single oil painted two years previously, ***Remains of the Palace La Reine Blanche, Paris.*** In the same Society's second winter exhibition, Holland had an oil entitled ***View of the Thames Below Greenwich***, another simply called ***Landscape*** and a water-colour ***View on the***

Ravensbourne, a subject which he later re-painted in oils. By this time he had been exhibiting for ten years, and some indication of his progress can be seen from the fact that in the first five years he had 18 works hung, all of which were either of fruit, flowers or nature studies, while in the last five the number had increased to 39, of which around half were landscapes or architectural subjects.

His painting efforts that year were again centred on the Greenwich area, and one result was the only Holland portrait ever accepted by the Royal Academy, *Gypsy*, which was in the 1834 exhibition. The British Institution took *Nelson Square Greenwich, Scene on the Darent* and another *View of London from Blackheath*, which was an oil. The Society of British Artists accepted three oils, including a large and very impressive study of the newly built (in 1828) *Hyde Park Corner and Constitution Arch*, displayed in The Tate Gallery just before the First World War and now in the Museum of London, plus a water-colour entitled *Evening*. In their final winter exhibition that year, James was represented by two more works entitled **Evening** - one oil, one water-colour - together with three further water-colours. These showed that he had spent some time along the South Coast developing his technique on marine subjects, and were entitled *Coast View, Sea View* and *Shipping, Bathing Machines, Etc.* He had ventured as far west as Arundel, since the British Museum possesses a pencil sketch dated that year of the *Fitzalan Sepulchral Chapel* which is in the castle there.

This was obviously a very busy time for Holland, since he also undertook his first visit to Scotland (even in those days still quite an adventure). From dated works he can be seen to have travelled via Warwick and once north of the border, to have done some work along the River Tay. Much closer to home, he also made a major effort in central London, especially in Westminster Abbey. All this work was rewarded with Holland's election to the Society of Painters in Water-colours on 9 February 1835, together with one Valentine Bartholomew, (who ultimately failed to live up to his promise). This was the beginning of a long, sometimes stormy, relationship with the Society, which was to gain the Royal prefix twelve years after his death.

His exhibiting record for 1835 was once again quite impressive, despite the fact that this year he missed out at the Royal Academy. The British Institution had an oil of *The Confessor's Chapel, Westminster Abbey* (of which an 1834 water-colour version can be seen in the Cecil Higgins Gallery in Bedford), plus oils of *St.Mary's Chapel, Warwick* and *The Palace of Phillipe le Bel, Paris*. The Society of British Artists displayed another *Coast Scene* oil and a different version of *The Confessor's Chapel*, while the Water-colour Society hung no fewer than six of his works in their Pall Mall galleries. There were two nature studies, views of *Greenwich* and *Charing Cross, On the River Tay*, and *An Old Mill at Blackheath*. The last named gained Holland his first press notice, when the Literary Gazette for the 9th of May 1835 commented that this water-colour was *"an excellent example of old age in picturesque objects."*

Doubtless inspired by his increasing success - and presumably wealth - James had been planning a long and arduous return to the Continent. He must have felt that his family was now old enough to enable him to get away for a time; his eldest daughter Elizabeth was now nearly fourteen, Emma was almost twelve, and his only

James Holland's passport details, Hotel Europe,Geneva, together with those of fellow artist Edward Ellis.

surviving son Thomas was ten. Holland's ultimate goal was to get to Venice, probably he had initially been inspired to go there by Bonington, and it is thought he started his journey towards the end of July, once the London exhibition season had got underway. He was accompanied on this journey by fellow artist Edward Ellis, who at 25 was ten years his junior, and after crossing the Channel, they set out for Paris, then on to Geneva where they stayed at the plush Hotel de Europe from 26 October. Geneva city archives record that on 29 October the travellers were issued with passports to enable them to continue their journey to Milan from whence they progressed to Verona and finally Venice, a city with which James obviously fell in love, returning there many times until just a few short years before his death.

A contemporary engraving of Venice

He painted Venice profusely in both oils and water-colours, and there are some documented criticisms that much of his work here lacked the touch and style of the younger Holland. The author disagrees with this view, finding much of his Venetian work quite stunning in its vibrancy of colour and delicateness of touch, although the water-colours were undoubtedly the more successful of the two mediums he used here. One of his first Venetian works, *A Side Canal, Venice,* painted on this 1835 trip, is in the Fitzwilliam Museum, Cambridge. By late autumn he was on his way home, stopping in Geneva to stay again at the Hotel de Europe in mid November. While here he painted a portrait *Peasant Woman at Geneva,* believed to still be in private hands. It is worth noting at this point that a Venice water-colour auctioned at Sotheby's in 1996 bore the date 1836, but there is no other evidence to suggest he returned there in that year and this was probably simply the year in which he completed this particular work.

From Geneva, Holland travelled on to Paris before arriving back at Union Place to find, it would seem, that all had not been well at home during his lengthy absence. Yet again, tragedy was to strike the male Holland line for on 14 December 1835, which can only have been a short while after James's return, his ten year old son Thomas was buried at St. Alfege's Church in Greenwich; the cause of his death has not been discovered. Thus in the fifteen years which had elapsed since his arrival in London, he had married, fathered three sons all of whom were now dead, and been widowed. The family now consisted of just himself and his two daughters; Elizabeth Ann and Emma Lavinia, and despite James's increasing financial comfort, the task of bringing them up without the guiding hand of their mother must have been onerous indeed.

A contemporary engraving of Paris

However, it seems that at some time during this tragic period, a family had come into Holland's life which was having a profound effect on him. This was George and Charlotte Martha Morrant, and their three daughters, who lived in Maiden Lane off The Strand. George was a floorcloth maker and printer, and a partner in a firm called Sargon and Mann's in Camden Town. There is a possibility that there was some relationship between the Morrants and James' wife Elizabeth. If this was the case, and they were around to help when all the illnesses and deaths first struck, this could certainly explain how he was able to spend so much time away on painting expeditions, since he would be secure in the knowledge that his young children were in safe hands. Undoubtedly the two families were very close, as evidenced by the fact that James lies buried with Charlotte and her daughter

Mary Ann, who is the first member of the family known to have had a close connection with him. Certainly by 1838 when she was twenty eight years of age, and possibly much earlier, Mary was housekeeping for him.

James had also come into contact with Mary's younger sister who was born in 1817, baptised on 15 June that year at St.Marylebone, and named Charlotte Martha after her mother. This was the young lady who was destined to become the artist's companion and lover. The earliest stages of their relationship only recently came to light with the discovery of an interesting entry in the record of baptisms in the parish of St.Mary's Lambeth for December 1835. On the 20th day of that month, just six days after Thomas William Holland had been buried in Greenwich, one James Holland, son of James and Charlotte Morrant, was baptised. The father's profession was given as "painter" and the address was Carlisle Square. This seems certain to have been our Holland, the likelihood of another James and Charlotte tied in with the names Holland and especially Morrant, which is unusual anyway, plus a father with the same profession, seems pretty remote. The address could well have been one to which George Morrant had taken the family, or perhaps that of another relative, given that Charlotte would have only been eighteen years old at the time. Unfortunately nothing further is known of this child, and Charlotte cannot be proved to re-appear in James's life for some time.

Perhaps then, domestic turmoil was one reason why 1836 was a lean year for Holland at the exhibitions, despite the large amount of material he must have brought back from the Continent. The Royal Academy showed Greenwich Hospital, a work which was much admired and which was eventually to be presented to the hospital, before passing to the National Maritime Museum in Greenwich, who still have it today among their small collection of Holland's. The British Institution had one of his now increasingly rare flower paintings, the Society of British Artists had a water-colour of Frankfurt which was painted during the 1835 journey, and the Water-colour Society showed the first of a great many exhibited Venice studies.

Meanwhile he continued to find new scenes in London to paint. The Athenaeum Club, which had opened in 1824 in Waterloo Place just off Pall Mall, was visited to produce a fine oil of the superbly appointed main reading room, which the club still possesses to this day. The Athenaeum was renowned as a popular haunt of artists, politicians, scientists and literary people among its 1,200 members, and was ranked amongst the foremost of all the London gentlemen's

The Athenaeum Club (The Queen's London)

clubs. Although there is no evidence that Holland ever aspired to actually join their ranks, it is likely that he was at least a not infrequent visitor.

This same year saw James paying his first visit to the imposing Knole House near Sevenoaks in Kent, the country seat, then as now, of the Sackville family. It is thought that he was first invited there as the result of being commissioned to produce illustrations for a guide book to the house and grounds. Indeed there is an 1839 Visitor's Guide to Knole by John H.Brady in the local history section of Sevenoaks Library, which contains several unaccredited studies of the house which

Knole House

seem to show James's hand in their style. Whatever in fact started the Knole connection, James was to become a regular house guest over many years, with dated works showing that he was at least there several times throughout the 1840s and again as late as 1865. Most of the major rooms within the house were painted, and although none of his pictures remain there today, there are two at nearby Sissinghurst Castle - which has family connections with Knole - and one in the Stoke City Museum and Art Gallery collection. It has been suggested by previous researchers into James's life that he gave painting lessons to Queen Victoria; although this claim has not been substantiated, it is interesting to note that the Queen was also a regular guest at Knole, usually visiting Lady Delawarr - was

An illustration from the visitor's guide to Knole published in 1839.

this where the supposed tutoring take place? He is certainly thought to have tutored members of the Sackville family during his visits.

While in Kent, Holland journeyed to the coast to stay with "Billy" Hunt, who because of poor health, spent extended periods by the sea. This gave James the opportunity to hone his skills with coastal and shipping scenes, and to master the often elusive technique of satisfactorily painting water, which was to serve him so well in his later Venetian studies. Also during that same year he visited Scotland twice, North Wales, Devon and East Anglia, so must have had a large amount of material to keep him busy in his studio over the winter. In addition, he was by now tutoring quite a number of pupils and earning a fair income from both teaching and book illustrations, for which he was becoming increasingly in demand, due not only to his skill but also to his having earned a reputation for always producing work on time. He seems to have been an astute business man, and was obviously planning his finances carefully to allow for all the Continental expeditions he was about to undertake.

The Cartoon Gallery, Knole, Kent
James Holland, Watercolour, Sept 1841. The Potteries Museum and Art Gallery, Stoke on Trent.

CHAPTER FOUR
THE SECOND FAMILY

In 1837, the most important commission to date came Holland's way. The Landscape Annual was a publication for travellers, which concentrated on a different country each year. There had developed a general widening of the avenues of travel throughout Europe, and this was followed by an intense interest in visiting new countries. Accordingly, a whole generation of artists earned their living by producing drawings of their Continental tours which were then engraved for inclusion in traveller's companions. The recent innovation of steel engraving plates allowed thousands of impressions of such volumes, enabling them to sell for a guinea or less.

In this year the chosen location for the Landscape Annual was Portugal and James was asked to provide all the illustrations. He set out in May, and probably took one of the steam packets George the Fourth or Duke of York direct to Lisbon

A Channel steam packet

where he arrived in the first week in June. From here he continued a few miles further west to the Os Pisoes (The Fulling Mill) Hotel in Cintra (now Sintra), kept by one Madam de Belam, who was in fact born in Hoxton, London. Her father had travelled to Spain many years before to sell merchandise, but had been attacked by bandits and robbed. Unable to pay his way home, he found work in a hotel before becoming a manager and then eventually owning one of his own. His daughter joined him and they went on to own hotels in Seville and both Lisbon and Cintra in Portugal. The daughter had then married a Colonel de Belem who had fought in Napoleon's army.

The hotel was renowned among travellers for its English style and for its food, being featured a few years later in the Reverend William Robertson's *Journal of a Clergyman*. James must have felt comfortably at home there - a water-colour he painted of it can be found in the Walker Art Gallery in Liverpool - and from its windows he was able to paint the nearby Moorish Palace. By the first of July, he had undertaken the long and arduous trek north to Oporto, but it seems he almost

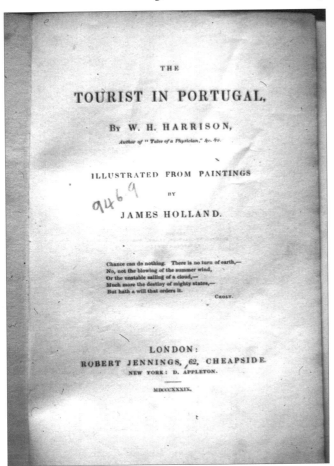

Title page from "Tourist in Portugal".

Leiria
from "Tourist in Portugal".
James Holland, sketch.

Os Pisôes, (The Fulling Mill) Cintra. James Holland, Watercolour, 1837. Victoria and Albert Museum.
The hotel where James stayed and was taken ill.

A photograph of Os Pisôes (The Fulling Mill), Sintra 1993.

immediately fell quite seriously ill, although the exact nature of the illness is not known. At any event, he was certainly back at the Cintra hotel by the 9th and from dated works it can be deduced that he travelled little if at all for the next two weeks.

Madam de Belem took good care of Holland and gradually nursed him back to health. She had a nine year old daughter called Rosalie, with whom James was apparently quite taken, for he gave her a drawing of the hotel, saying that she reminded him of his own daughters. Rosalie kept this picture for more than seventy years, before, as Mrs Augustus Reynolds, giving it to the Victoria and Albert Museum in 1909, just two years before her death. It was reproduced in the Connoisseur in June 1925.

Once he was back on his feet, James set about the task in hand, with his travels taking him first the short distance to Mafra, then on to Alcobaco, Batalha, Coimbra, and Leiria for the glorious medieval castle, Mafra again, Porto de Moz and of course Lisbon, where he painted particularly extensively. On his study of St. Joseph's church in the capital, he added a pencilled note "destroyed by the earthquake", a reference to a major earthquake which had hit the area some 40 or so years earlier. By late August James had returned to Oporto to complete his interrupted work there, and he appears to have set out for home in early September. In addition to the Walker Gallery, works from this trip can today be found in the Victoria and Albert Museum, the Fitzwilliam in Cambridge, and the Stoke collection.

The ground-work for the commission at last complete, Holland returned home to Greenwich, and then faced the task of completing the 18 chosen works for the engravers, (the completed book *The Tourist in Portugal,* with text by W.H.Harrison, was finally published in 1839). This task, coupled with his longer than expected

Leiria, Portugal
James Holland, Watercolour, 1837. Victoria and Albert Museum.

Cintra, Portugal
James Holland, Watercolour, 1837.
Victoria and Albert Museum.

Part of Old Treasury, Lisbon
James Holland, Watercolour, 2nd June 1837.
Victoria and Albert Museum.

stay in Portugal, left him with little time to prepare works for the coming exhibition season. In fact 1838 was to see him show only three, the lowest number since 1827. His Royal Academy offering was a flower painting, the British Institution had an oil of **Verona** from the 1835 trip and the Water-colour Society showed a drawing from the 1837 travels.

The summer of 1838, which witnessed the coronation of Queen Victoria in June, brought yet another death to Holland's family. His step-father - and possibly natural father - Timothy Edge had been a long-time sufferer from asthma, and it had finally got the better of him. He died at Waterloo Road, Burslem on 4 August and was buried in the Holland family grave in Burslem churchyard; James probably attended the funeral. He must have recovered his own health quite well by this time, since he was able to set out in September on yet another extensive trip, starting in Lisbon, before crossing Spain into France and then on to Venice. He worked hard on the results of this trip, with the result that the following year he showed no fewer than seven oils and five water-colours, all of Continental scenes. The Royal Academy had a particularly fine view entitled **Lisbon from Port Brandes,** which drew the attention of Thackeray who, writing in Fraser's Magazine described him as a welcome addition to the landscape painters, *"not quite so glib and smooth as those from more practised hands but they are, perhaps, more like nature and certainly less mannered than the excellent, though exaggerated, performances of the seniors in the art."* One of his exhibited water-colours that year, **The Monastery of Alcobaca,** also drew comment in the Athenaeum; *"a picturesque composition of fantastic architecture in a state of decay, which Mr. Beckford ought to purchase."*

As for family life, it seems to have been at about this time that the younger Charlotte Morrant came back into James's life. Although he was then 38 years of age, and she only 21, they got on well together, with Charlotte expressing an interest in James's work, and he offering to teach her painting. In the summer of 1839 they spent much time together, especially in the large garden behind 3 Union Place and in the additional garden land which Holland had rented since the previous year from nearby Morden College, which was actually not a college at all but an almshouse built by Wren in 1700. He seemed to return to his painting roots here for a time, producing many flower paintings which were still in his studio when he died, perhaps reflecting the more private and intimate circumstances under which they were painted.

James left for Venice again in August, by which time Charlotte would no doubt have confided in her sister Mary - still the housekeeper - that she was once more pregnant by him. James too must have known before he left, for his trip was shorter than usual, and he returned to handle what must have been a very difficult situation. Presumably in an attempt to save face, Charlotte was spirited away to lodgings at 4 Sion Place, East Street, Newington and at six o'clock in the morning on 14 February 1840, gave birth to a baby girl. She was registered as Louisa Charlotte Morrant, with her mother being given, rather curiously, as Charlotte Morrant, formerly James, the father being listed as James Morrant, painter. The registration was made six weeks after the birth on the very last day allowable by law, by Charlotte herself. No doubt the removal of Charlotte from Union Place, and all the secrecy with the names, was brought about by a desire to protect James's legitimate daughters Elizabeth and Emma from any whiff of scandal. By this time they were aged eighteen and sixteen respectively, and explaining a baby step-sister in those days, would have been difficult to say the least, and certainly damaging to their father's standing. It is also conceivable that, given the Morrants' modest circumstances especially when compared to James, there may even have been a degree of blackmail to keep his personal life private.

Despite all this, Holland had eleven works hung that summer, of which no fewer than eight were oils. Although he missed out on the Royal Academy, both the British Institution and the Society of British Artists showed four apiece. Thackeray again penned comment, this time on Holland's **Milan Cathedral** at the Society, which he described as *"a large, raw, clever picture."* With the tricky family circumstances to consider, James stayed in and around London and Greenwich that summer, one of the results being a further water-colour of **The Confessor's Chapel at Westminster.** Indeed it would seem that he was still using studio premises in central London at this time, since the records of his account at the London and

Westminster Bank in Stratford Place off Oxford Street, give his address as 31 Manchester Street. That autumn, he submitted once again to the siren call of Venice, and whilst there produced the water-colour which now resides in the Manchester City Art Gallery. In December, not long after his return, Charlotte's father George died of apoplexy at the Sargon and Mann works.

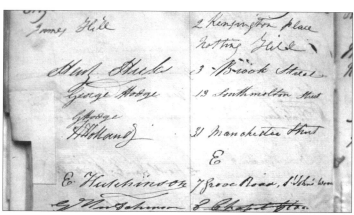

James's entry in the records of the London and Westminster Bank, Stratford Place.

In 1841 it was time for the ten-yearly population census and for the first time the ages and occupations of everyone in the household were required to be given. There was naturally some suspicion regarding the motives behind these questions and when the census enumerator called at Union Place, James obviously decided to be difficult. The visitor wrote *"Mr Holland thinks the Christian names are not required"* and had to settle for listing initials only. Holland told him he was 35 when he was actually five years older and said that Elizabeth and Emma were fifteen year old twins - one was nearly twenty and the other eighteen. Mary Morrant was given as being 25 when she was 30, and a 15 year old girl servant completed the household. There is no sign of Charlotte and the baby, who were presumably still away at Sion Place - or did he simply choose not to mention them?

Demand for James' artistic talents continued to increase, and during this time he was commissioned to paint a large oil of Edward Langford of Blackheath, together with his wife and daughter in the drawing room of their home, **The Langford Family in their Drawing Room**. This work was auctioned out of the Langford family by Sotheby's in 1989, and a label on the reverse in the artist's hand, acknowledged receipt of £50 in payment - a considerable sum in those days.

After another summer visit to Knole House, the usual Continental trip came around again that autumn. James left from Dover and while awaiting his ship on 31 August, painted the water-colour now in the Fitzwilliam Museum. He travelled on to Antwerp, where he painted *St. Jacques Church, Antwerp,* then to Paris and Geneva before finally reaching Venice once again. The results were seen in 1842 when he exhibited eight works, of which five were water-colours from this trip. The three oils shown included *View on the Ravensbourne, Kent* at the Royal Academy, which was afterwards kept and treasured by Charlotte, before eventually being handed down to a son-in-law. Doubtless it reminded her of happy times with James.

From a professional viewpoint, 1842 was a difficult year for Holland. He did not travel abroad that autumn as was his custom, and then on 30 November he delivered a bolt from the blue. On that day he wrote to the Water-colour Society to resign his associate membership, an extraordinary step causing quite a stir in contemporary art circles, and one which has never been satisfactorily explained. One possible explanation was that despite being in every exhibition in the eight years following his election to the society, he remained an associate member rather than having the coveted full membership. At this time the society was actually bestowing this honour only sparingly, largely due to its own rules restricting numbers, which had the unfortunate effect of keeping out much of the outstanding talent of the day. If this were the reason, it is conceivable that what Holland may have perceived as a snub was sufficient to force his resignation.

Randall Davies F.S.A., writing in the society's annual volume for 1929/30, suggested that Holland possessed a *"difficult if not arrogant temperament"*, but this view is not borne out by others who recorded him as being amicable and blessed with a lively sense of fun. Indeed, faced with criticism by John Ruskin which many might have regarded as unfounded and pedantic, the critic himself recorded Holland's reaction as *"singularly good-humoured."*

Another possible explanation was that James was hoping for election to the Royal Academy, and thus may have felt that he needed to dispel any thoughts that he was primarily a water-colourist. Hugh Stokes, writing in Walker's Quarterly in 1927, mentions a letter from Holland to Edward Magrath, Secretary of the Athenaeum Club dated 24 April 1837, in which the artist says; *"It is more a want of confidence in my own powers that has hitherto kept me from sending to the R.A., than to any want of faith in their disposition to do justice to any talented artist. I will henceforth devote myself to painting, and look forward with hope to something worthy of notice."* - hardly the words of an arrogant man. Edward Magrath was a friend of James's, buying several of his pictures, and it may well have been he who suggested to the artist that he try for election to the R.A.

However, the thought that he did not wish to be regarded as mainly a water-colourist is hard to reconcile with the fact that in the eight years leading up to the writing of that letter, he had exhibited oils and water-colours in almost equal numbers. The fact that he missed the Royal Academy exhibition in 1837 may have been what prompted the letter, leading back to the first suggestion that his resignation from the Water-colour Society was most likely to have been a result of frustration with his lack of progress within it. Despite this, by the time of his resignation, he was producing far more water-colours than oils.

The British Institution and Society of British Artists continued to serve him well at this time and in the year following his resignation he was elected to the Society of British Artists. He also received the following glowing notice from Ruskin in his Modern Painters publication of that year, *"I have seen, some seven years ago, works by J. Holland which were I think, as near perfection as water-colour can be carried - for bona fide truth, refined and finished to the highest degree."*

St. Peter's, Broadstairs.
A contemporary engraving of Rural Kent

During that same summer of 1843 he worked a great deal in and around London and rural Kent, painting the delightful oil **View on the Ravensbourne**, which appeared in a London auction house as recently as 1996. He also fitted in a visit to Knole, before crossing the Channel to Rotterdam en route to Venice for the early autumn. The pattern was repeated in 1844, with dated works showing that he travelled to Venice that year via Geneva and Verona, and seems to have concentrated almost exclusively on water-colour.

Holland's financial situation was by now very comfortable since he was carrying out a good deal of painting for direct sale to collectors and had a substantial number of fee-paying pupils, doubtless still renting central studios for the purpose. He must have decided that once again he needed to move back to the centre of things and accordingly in March 1845 he said goodbye to Union Place and took his two daughters and Mary Ann Morrant back north of the river. They settled in an elegant and spacious four storey Regency terrace house at 11 Osnaburgh Street (named after King George III's son HRH Frederick, Bishop of Osnabruck). This was near Regents Park and lead off from The New Road (now Euston Road), near the still prominent Holy Trinity Church. Long since demolished, Holland's house stood on the spot now covered by number 32. At the rear there was a single storey building which he used as his studio. His next door neighbour was the sculptor William Behnes, and next but one on either side were fellow artists William Darby and Henry Cousins. Five doors up the street was another sculptor, John Henry Foley R.A. and at the other end of the row lived the miniaturist William Essex and his artist son, also William.

James had certainly achieved his desire to be back amongst the artists' set, but equally as importantly, did this move enable him to unite both his families? By now Louisa was five years old and James's legitimate daughters were 24 and 22, ages at which they could be expected to be rather more understanding of their father's liaison with Charlotte. It seems highly likely that she and the child would now have

Head of Lake Geneva. James Holland, Oil, 1843. Graves Art Gallery, Sheffield.

left Newington to join James permanently in his far more luxurious surroundings; the fact that Mary Ann was still housekeeping suggests that the inter-family relationships had been kept on a fairly even keel. In fact, Mary Ann's younger sister Sarah Ellis was also a frequent visitor to the house.

Before he left Greenwich, he had submitted his summer exhibition works, gaining six acceptances from the Society of British Artists and five from the British Institution, so presumably feeling well satisfied with his efforts and more settled in his domestic affairs, he planned his next Continental trip, perhaps during a brief stay at Knole, finally setting out in mid August. He was accompanied for the first time by Hercules Brabazon, a young artist whom Holland had taken under his wing, and this was to be the first of many such trips they shared. By the twenty second of the month they were in Paris, where he painted **The Rue St. George** on the 23rd, travelling on to Dordrecht before

Rotterdam - a contemporary engraving.

arriving in Rotterdam by 23 September. They set off again the following month to Delft, Geneva, Verona and finally Venice, little knowing that all was far from well at home.

On 3 October the family doctor, Dr Charles Chinner Fuller, was summoned from his practice at nearby 160 Albany Street to attend to a feverish Elizabeth Ann. The news was grave, despite the fact that both Holland's daughters had been vaccinated when young, Elizabeth had contracted smallpox. Letters were no doubt hastily despatched to the Continent in the vain hope that James could be reached and return home in time, but all to no avail. He was away from home until at least the end of October, and in all probability was in Geneva on the 12th when Elizabeth died,

Elizabeth died from smallpox, nine days after falling ill.

just nine days after falling ill. Her death made a lasting impression on little Louisa who, although she was no doubt kept away from the infection during the crisis, knew her step-sister as "auntie" and in the twilight of her long life still treasured a miniature of her.

Sarah was sent to register the death, and since Holland was still away, the ladies of the house had to make the necessary funeral arrangements themselves. Elizabeth was taken the short distance to the burial ground at St.James's, Hampstead Road on 18 October, the ceremony being conducted by the Reverend Doctor Henry Stebbing. The cemetery is near Euston station, and is today a small public open space, with most of the headstones - including that of Elizabeth, her baby brother James and her mother - cleared away.

James was painting in Rotterdam and Delft in the last few days of October, still blissfully unaware of the troubles at home, and so must have been devastated by what he found on his eventual return. His winter studio work and subsequent exhibiting effort the following summer bear testimony to the strain he must have been under. He returned to the Royal Academy for the first time in four years with a Knole House study which had been painted at least two years earlier, had three oils from the 1845 trip in the British Institution and six further works in the Society of British Artists. The lack lustre effort drew the attention of the artist David Cox who, in a letter to a friend, remarked *"Holland not so good"*, it was hardly surprising. Nevertheless, in Cox's reviews, James was one of only eleven named artists, among such notables as Francis Danby, De Wint, Fielding, Harding, Pyne and Turner - good company indeed.

This same year 1845, also saw the passing of his good friend John Scarlett Davis, who had known James almost from the time he arrived from Burslem, and who had accompanied him on his first Continental journey 14 years before. There was a self-portrait of Davis in Holland's home at the time of his own demise in 1870.

Charlotte. An 1853 oil by James Holland entitled *Nellie Nick*.

CHAPTER FIVE
DAYS WITH CHARLOTTE

Some years after the traumatic events of that early autumn in 1845, James painted one of his very few portraits, an oil entitled Nellie Nick. It shows the full length figure of an elegant, dark haired young woman who is believed to actually be his partner Charlotte Morrant. She was certainly a very handsome lady and it is easy to see why the artist was attracted to her. The fact that they became devoted to each other cannot be disputed, although both Victorian convention and James's painting journeys meant that there were extended enforced separations, and the relationship was probably quite stormy at times.

During the summer of 1846, Holland returned to Knole House once more, before going back to Portugal and the de Belem hotel at Cintra. On the way he found time to paint evening studies of *The White Cliffs of Dover* and *The French Coast from Dover*, whilst awaiting passage on 23 August. This seems to have been more of a restful trip than a working one, for there are few dated works to show for it, although Sheffield's Grave's Gallery has a pencil and wash drawing of the *St. Honrius Cave at Cintra*. Perhaps Charlotte travelled with him, and they simply wanted some time away together after all the sadness. Whatever the case, the return to England was met with even further family troubles.

James's mother Martha had suffered from asthma for three years, and his step-brother Timothy Edge wrote to say that she was getting steadily worse, with increasingly severe attacks. By this time Martha was seventy and was still living at Barnfield, Wolstanton, with an old servant by the name of Ann Scarratt looking after her. Finally in the early hours of 21 January 1847 she succumbed to a particularly bad attack, and died at 4.00am. Holland travelled north for the funeral, and Martha was buried in the same family plot in a corner of Burslem churchyard that already held her husband Timothy, her father, mother and grandmother. Not long after his return, Holland marked Louisa's seventh birthday by painting a small commemorative pastel circle for her, which he inscribed *"To Too-Roo-Itity"* - two generations later, Louisa was still known to her grandchildren as Too-Roo.

That year Holland had fourteen oils on exhibition, the highest number in any year of his long career. There were two at the Royal Academy, the first time for nearly twenty years that they had taken more than a single work from him. The British Institution took three Venice studies plus one from his Dutch travels, and the Society of British Artists had eight, five of Venice and three of the Kent coast. The Society also paid him the compliment that year of electing him to be one of two honorary auditors, alongside Alfred Clint, son of George Clint R.A. In spite of this, it seems that Holland was in some way becoming disenchanted with the Society.

In 1841, F.V. Hurlestone was re-elected President of the Society for the second time, a position he was to hold until 1870. Previously, a new President had been elected annually, and Holland disliked this new situation, holding the view that art organisations should change and grow to keep their ideas alive. He showed seven more oils at the Society's 1848 exhibition, but then resigned and was not to exhibit there again. The 1848 season saw him have four oils hung at the British Institution, but he had now exiled himself from two of the major art organisations of the day, and must have felt somewhat away from the centre of things at this time.

He set off on his customary autumn trip, and spent some time in Rotterdam, but if he had intended to travel on to Venice, events there quickly put paid to any such plans. Ruled by Austria, the Venetians had long resented this foreign domination, and elected to fall behind the cry to unite Italy. Finally in 1848 the Venetians rose in arms in rebellion against their Austrian masters. The uprising lasted for eighteen months, during which time the city was besieged, with both hunger and plague afflicting the population. Thus although James produced two Venetians dated that year, they must have been studio works based on earlier sketches, and his Continental travels do not appear to have gone beyond Rotterdam. The result was a showing at the 1849 Royal Academy of two works, both entitled *Rotterdam - an October Morning*.

In that summer, while the nation honoured Lord Nelson by erecting his memorial in Trafalgar Square, James and Charlotte set out together for a holiday in the West Country. The Stoke City Art Gallery has a water-colour of the popular resort of Ilfracombe done on this journey, and they seem to have based themselves

during July and August in the pretty Exmoor fishing village of Lynmouth, which the poet Shelley had enthused about, after a visit with his young bride back in 1812, and where James produced another water-colour which is now in the British Museum. By September they were back in Kent, and James spent some time at Knole House, from where he travelled to paint at least three views of Walmer town and its magnificent castle, the official residence of the Lord Warden of the Cinque Ports, the Duke of Wellington. That winter he concentrated on a very large oil of Rotterdam which was at one time in the collection of Sir Joseph Beecham, and also finished another oil depicting *A Morning Concert at the Palace of Philip le Bel* in Paris. His efforts were rewarded with no fewer than three works in the 1850 Royal Academy, including the morning concert picture and his first Venetian view to be hung there. He once again came to the attention of the critic Ruskin, who commented *"Mr Holland is alike skilled in oil and water-colour painting; and the amateur has long ere this admired on the walls of our*

Cottages at Lynmouth.
Lynmouth.
Contemporary engraving.

exhibitions, his rich and luminous colouring, his sunny buildings of his favourite Venetian architecture, his clear waters, and his deep Italian skies. This painter claims, as a right, to take his place in any gallery of English landscape, etc."

He revisited his old haunts around Greenwich early that year, painting a view of the hospital which is now in the National Maritime Museum, and once he had sorted out his exhibition pictures, he and Charlotte left London on their travels

View of Naples
James Holland, watercolour. The Potteries Museum and Art Gallery, Stoke on Trent.

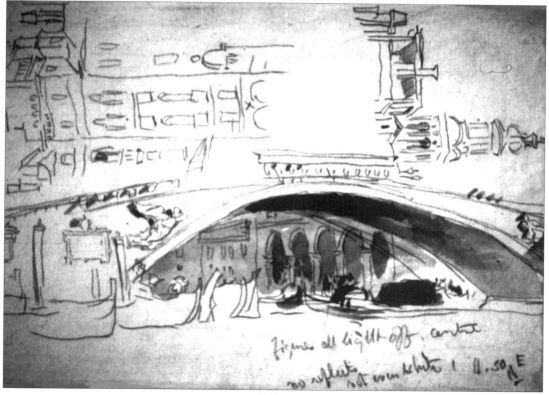

Venice
James Holland, sketch, 1850. Private Collection.

again. This time they headed for North Wales, and it was probably during this trip that Charlotte became pregnant again. They headed for Betws-y-Coed in Snowdonia to paint the magnificent Swallow Falls, a popular attraction since their discovery by the artist David Cox during his 1805-6 tour. They also visited Beddgelert near Caernarfon, an especially beautiful little village in the mountains at the meeting point of two rivers.

Not long after returning home, James left for the Continent, painting several water-colours of **Rouen's Clock Tower** and churches during mid August, including one of **St. Maclou** which is now in the Fitzwilliam Museum. He travelled on to Normandy, where he made several sketches of costume and scenery, Paris, Geneva and Rome before making what was probably his only visit to Corfu where he did preliminary sketches for an oil which he completed the following year. The extended trip, accompanied by his friend Hercules Brabazon, then took him across the Mediterranean to Egypt, where he painted a water-colour of the newly built harbour at Alexandria. This work, the only one so far identified which marks the farthest extent of his travels, remains in private hands. However, a water-colour of Luxor painted by his companion, surfaced in a London saleroom in 1997 and although undated, may well have been painted on this same journey.

Alexandria - a contemporary engraving.

James finally returned home early in the new year of 1851, to discover that Charlotte was now heavily pregnant, and once again, for whatever reason, she left Osnaburgh Street for the confinement and returned to be with her 63 year old mother who was living over a shop at 11 South Street, Clerkenwell. The census returns for that year give us these facts, and also show that eleven year old Louisa, who carried the surname Morrant, went with her mother, who described herself as an *"artist in painting."* None of her work seems to have survived, but two anonymous water-colours among the artist's effects following his death, may have been Charlotte's work. Back at the family home, Holland's census return listed the household as comprising himself, his daughter Emma, Mary Morrant (described as a visitor) and a servant from the North Country. James again lied about his age, saying that he was fifty when he was actually two years older, and described himself as a widower. There was no sign on this occasion of Mary's sister Sarah.

Charlotte's baby was born on 13 April 1851 and was christened Alice Morrant

Holland; James and Charlotte still seemed undecided about what surname to use for their children. He made the registration himself, giving his correct name and occupation as the father, but listing his address as 11 South Street, Clerkenwell. The mother was entered as Charlotte Martha Holland, formerly Morrant, but in fact for the first nine years of her life, the child was brought up as Alice Morrant.

He again left for the Continent in the summer, being in Rouen in July and thence via Geneva to Genoa for September and October. He seems to have regularly used three routes to Italy; via Paris and Geneva to Genoa, Verona and Venice; via Lucerne, the Gotthard Pass and down either Lake Lugano or Lake Maggiore, or via Frankfurt, Munich and Austria. The favoured route from dated works seems to have been via Geneva and there is a vague hint of another possible relationship there. One of James's grandsons, whose mother was the 1840 child Louisa, said she had told him that she knew of a cousin in Geneva. It seems highly improbable that Holland could have carried on such a long-distance relationship, only visiting for a few weeks in the autumn and then not every year, but could this be why he never married Charlotte? We shall never know.

On this 1851 trip he still did not return to Venice, which must have been quite a wrench given his love for the place, which he was to express so eloquently a few years later. During the late 1980s, a very small Venetian water-colour in the Holland collection at the Stoke City Art Gallery, was removed from its outsize frame to reveal that it was in fact painted on a sheet of notepaper. On the reverse was the following poem written in Holland's hand and signed by him:

Venice

I stood in Venice on the Bridge of Sighs,
A palace and a prison on each hand,
I saw from out the wave her structures rise,
As from the stroke of the enchanted wand.
A thousand years their cloudy wings expand
Around me, and a dying Glory smiles,
O'er the far times, when many a subject land,
Look'd to the winged Lirbis marble piles,
When Venice sat in state, throned on her hundred isles.

She looks a sea Cybele, fresh from ocean,
Rising with her strata of proud towers,
All airy distance, with majestic motion,
A ruler of the waters and their powers,
And such she was; her daughters had their dowery,
From spoils of nations, and the exhaustless East,
Pour'd in her lap all gems in sparkling showers,
In purple she was robed, and of her feast,
Monarchs partook, and deemed their dignity increased.

JH   March 6/56

At the 1852 Royal Academy summer exhibition, Holland had two works accepted again, **Tomb of the Scaligers at Verona** and **Effects after Rain, Venice,** while the British Institution had three oils. The autumn trip this time took him to Paris, Genoa, where he painted an oil of the city from the bay, and Geneva, where he did several water-colours. The 1853 Academy had just one exhibit **S. Pier da Arena, Geneva,** and the British Institution took four oils. Interestingly, for the first time this year, they listed in their catalogues the artist's asking prices for their works; only one of Holland's was thus quoted - presumably the others were painted for patrons who had loaned them - and this was **Salmon Trap, Glyn Lleddr** for which he was asking 100 guineas (£105).

This year saw him finally return to Venice, travelling via Rotterdam. The Leeds City Art Gallery has an oil of **The Piazza of San Marco** looking towards the statue, which was painted on this trip, as was the **Rotterdam Canal Scene** in the Harris Gallery at Preston. Another oil was **A View on the Grand Canal with the Rialto in the Distance**, which ended up in the F.J.Nettlefold collection, and was used as the basis for the scenery design by J.Halford Ross in Mr Nettlefold's production of Othello at London's Scala Theatre in 1919.

For their 1854 exhibition, which opened at the Pall Mall galleries in February, the British Institution took two Holland oils, one of **Venice** and the other of **Deal Beach**. The *Illustrated London News* saw fit to comment on the Deal picture *"There is considerable merit of intention in J.Holland's Deal Beach with a rolling sea on, and boats in the distance; but the water is rather hard, wants fluidity; and the colouring of the rainbow is excessive in intensity, and wants the evanescent ethereal character of atmospheric phenomena."* Clearly James's brilliant use of colour was not to everyone's liking.

The Royal Academy took a Rotterdam oil, but all was not well here in James's view. Despite his consistent exhibiting record of 31 pictures in 30 years, with no fewer than ten being shown in the last six years, he was once again passed over by the Academicians in his efforts to gain election as an Associate, and he seems to have decided to make no further effort here. (It is worth mentioning at this point that the Holland works exhibited at the Royal Academy in 1864 and 1865, which are often credited to James, were actually painted by John Holland, one of a father and son pair of artists from Nottingham, whose work has frequently been confused with his). The decision to divorce himself from the Royal Academy must have been a hard one to make, for as he was already estranged from the Water-colour Society, this would only leave the British Institution as a means of bringing his work to the public's attention.

Nevertheless, he certainly counted Royal Academicians amongst his close acquaintances, and during a dinner party in November 1854, recounted a story concerning JMW Turner, which seemed to indicate that they had spent time together on the Continent. The story told how Turner, who was fêted by his fellow artists during a lengthy stay in Rome, was persuaded against his will to put on an exhibition of his latest works before he left for home. Having no suitable frames available, Turner went out and bought a considerable length of marine rope, which he proceeded to cut and nail around the pictures as a substitute for frames.

Holland was now 55 years old, in comfortable circumstances, and perhaps no longer felt the burning ambition of old, so that autumn's Venice trip must have enabled a good deal of quiet reflection on the direction he wanted to take for the future. At the following year's British Institution he showed four oils; three priced, **Sunset** at 40 guineas, **The Rialto** 35 guineas, and **On the Grand Canal** 25 guineas. Interestingly, despite the fact that between 1847 and 1855 he exhibited 58 oils and no water-colours, dated works show that he actually painted more of the latter. Another product of that 1854 Venice trip was a small oil of the **Piazza di San Marco** which is now in the possession of the Royal Holloway College in Egham. Of particular interest is the inscription on the reverse, which reads, *"To Peter Potter*

Esq. This picture is a genuine work of Yours Very Truly James Holland, Jan 22, 1855."

In the summer of 1855 he travelled to Paris for the International Exhibition, where he received an honourable mention from the jury for his **Greenwich Hospital seen from the Thames**, a large untitled architectural work, and **Rotterdam**. While in France he stopped off once again at Rouen to paint **Rouen from the River**, which was still in his studio at the time of his death. Not long after returning home, he took Charlotte on another trip to North Wales, while Charlotte's mother looked after four year old Alice. The Cecil Higgin's Gallery in Bedford has a water-colour painted in Snowdonia on 18 September; the British Museum has **Nant Mill Caernarvonshire** from 26 September and they are also visited Conway.

Back in London, James again came under sustained pressure to rejoin the Water-colour Society. Since his resignation, the Society had been considerably enlivened by the election of the likes of Charles Bentley, William Callow, G.H.Dodgson, both the Fripps, John Gilbert, Samuel Palmer, T.M.Richardson and Francis Topham. The instigators of this latest attempt to make Holland rejoin the fold were Frederick Barton (later Sir), Joseph Jenkins, George Fripp and John Gilbert who was later to become the President of the Royal Water-colour Society and also to receive a knighthood. Realising that he still only had the British Institution taking his work, and certainly retaining a deep affection for the highly saleable water-colour medium to judge by the number he was still producing, James allowed his name to be put forward and on 11 February 1856 he was unanimously re-elected as an associate of the Society. The decision received fulsome praise from the art world, with the Art Journal commenting that *"Mr Holland has established for himself a high reputation by his beautiful Venetian subjects and must be looked upon as an important acquisition to the list of water-colour painters at this institution."*

The wheel had turned full circle, and Holland had returned to his roots.

A Cottage in N. Wales
James Holland, watercolour, 1855. Spink-Leger Pictures.

The nineteenth century pleasures of
London Life and Continental travel were
very much those of James Holland.
Some of the places he visited and loved
shown in engravings of the period

Venice

The Ducal Palace and Campanile. V

Geneva

Rouen

Innsbruck

CHAPTER SIX
PUBLIC ACCLAIM - DOMESTIC STRIFE

Holland's return to the Water-colour Society was marked in fine style at their Pall Mall exhibition of 1856. His six displayed works included three Venetians of which one was entitled **Moonlight**, and three painted in Genoa and the surrounding countryside. The Art Journal reviewed the exhibition and commented that James's **Market Day, Genoa** was *"a spirited sketch."* The British Institution still took his oils, including one of **Lynmouth** priced at 80 guineas and another of **Rouen** at 130 guineas which did not sell and was still in his studio when he died. Apart from his exhibiting success, this seems to have been a quiet year for the artist, as there are only two known works dated 1856, one depicting **A Glen in North Wales** and the other the **Grand Canal in Venice**. He did not travel abroad this year, so the Venetian must have been completed in the studio from earlier studies.

He again spent time on the Kent coast, as evidenced by a letter written that summer to a friend, now in the collection at the Royal water-colour Society: *"I returned home last night from Margate, where for the last 7 days I have been located, and very much enjoying the changeable weather, Thunder, Lightning, Hail and Rain! all four, the wind from the North East.....The sea leaped over the Piers into the harbour every 3rd or 5th wave........The bathing at Ramsgate was something exclusively English, and most particularly the reverse of all that our fair country women are said to perfect.........I shall now work for a short time and then think of where to go? and what to do? Dear North Wales! There my heart wil be, wheresoever I may wield the brush, ... the mountain side it will be, near Snowdon or on the coast. I have Betwys-y-Coed in my Portfolio, after a fashion."*

Early the following year, further recognition from the Water-colour Society came his way when he was awarded the much prized honour of being elected a full member, which resulted in his devoting considerable time and effort into helping with the Society's activities in whatever way he was able, for the rest of his life. They exhibited three of his works that summer, scenes in Rotterdam, Rouen and Venice and once again the Art Journal was moved to comment: *"All lovers of water-colour art must be gratified again to see the name of Mr. Holland in the Catalogue of this Society. How distasteful soever may have been his retirement"* (from the Society in 1842) *"it cannot have been otherwise than profitable to himself, judging from the force and freshness of the pictures he now exhibits."* His Rotterdam picture drew the remark, *"This is an unflinching broad daylight interpretation - an extremely difficult rendering of any subject, from the liability to fall into flatness. The materials are by no means of elevated character, but they are brought forward with elegant taste."* Once again the British Institution took two oils, both priced at 40 guineas and another, unidentified work was exhibited at Crystal Palace.

He undertook what was probably the most productive Continental painting trip of his life that year, travelling with Hercules Brabazon to Innsbruck, D'Ampezzo in the Tyrol, Genoa and Venice where, amongst other subjects, he painted Titian's birth-place at Capo de Cadore. There are many works from this trip in various collections today, including the National Museum of Wales in Cardiff, Liverpool's Walker Art Gallery, The Fitzwilliam in Cambridge, Leeds City

Art Gallery, the Laing Gallery in Newcastle, Manchester City Art Gallery, the British Museum and Bedford's Cecil Higgins collection. He returned to Osnaburgh St on the 15th November.

On New Year's Day, Holland presented an 1830 preliminary sketch of **Greenwich Hospital's Painted Hall** to a patron. The sketch is now in the Huntington collection in California, and is inscribed on the mount *"Mrs Hollier, with James Holland's kind regards, January 1st 1858."* One Richard Hollier later presented the finished work, which was completed in 1836, to the Commissioners of Greenwich Hospital.

Holland was in very good form during this period, and this was reflected in the press notices he received in 1858. The Water-colour Society showed two views on **Innsbruck**, one of **D'Ampezzo** and three of **Venice** and the Art Journal said *"Holland contributes three or four of the most fascinating drawings he has ever made."* They singled out the Innsbruck drawings for attention, commenting that they were *"broad and real in their emphatic expression of light"*, while one of the Venetians was *"elegant and brilliant without effort; it is a masterly tho' simple combination of...buildings...sky...and water. The work is beautiful in its simplicity, candid in its natural expression."*

The days of following Bonington's style were long past, but a strong echo remained, coupled with a brilliant use of colour which was all his own. He had given one of his D'Ampezzo water-colours to Brabazon, who copied it and kept it in his own collection right up until his death. However, the trade in techniques seems to have been working both ways by this time, as it has been suggested that Holland's **Venetian Island** done on this trip, shows an interesting variation in style which perhaps owes something to the pupil.

The British Institution now joined the ranks of those honouring Holland, by electing him to membership. He showed three oils there that year, **Fountain di San Giorgio, Genoa** priced at 160 guineas (£168), **Salmon Leap** and **The Glen, North Wales,** both at 100 guineas (£105), excellent money for those times, when a good bottle of wine could be bought for around two shillings (10 pence) a bottle.

James set out for Scotland for the third time that summer, doubtless starting from nearby Euston to take advantage of the newly completed West Coast railway line. He was to stay as a guest of one Colonel Inge in Inverness-shire during the annual grouse shooting season, and was accompanied by John Phillip who had been elected an Associate of the Royal Academy the previous year. Eighteen years younger than his travelling companion, Phillip was himself a Scotsman and shared Holland's love of rich colour in his painting. The two had met in Spain where Phillip spent several months each year on the advice of his doctor, with the result that to his fellow artists he was known as Phillip of Spain. Holland had two sketches of *Spanish Girls* and a view of *Braemar* by Phillip hanging in the house at Osnaburgh Street, together with a picture of **Scottish Cottages** which they painted between them. The only other jointly painted works which Holland is known to have been involved in, were three portraits for which he painted the backgrounds, and one E.U.Eddis painted the portraits themselves. The subjects were Edward Magrath, Secretary of the Athenaeum Club, plus the two artists, and all three works were still in the studio when James died.

Works completed by James on this 1858 Scottish journey included **Cannoc**

Burn, Glen Affric, Loch Benevian and various views on Colonel Inge's land, and not long after his return he set out again to Innsbruck and then on to Venice, where he painted the water-colour of the *Ospedale Civile* which is in the Victoria and Albert collection. The next year the *Cannoc Burn* work appeared as one of eight in the Water-colour Society exhibition and the Art Journal described it thus *"The subject is a deep, dark eddying pool in a limestone basin. A very powerful sketch, never touched apparently since it was put into the portfolio on the spot."* The British Institution accepted three oils, one from Scotland, one of *Venice* and one of *St.Lawrence's Church in Rotterdam.*

Earlier in the year the family had moved again, but only three doors along Osnaburgh Street to number 8, directly opposite the Holy Trinity Church, on a site now covered by a block of flats. The house was slightly smaller than number 11, but occupied a more open position. Who exactly was in the household is not clear, since there has been no mention of Charlotte for some time, but there is no reason to assume that she was not still with James.

Yet again in 1859, he undertook a very lengthy Continental trip, starting in Portugal for the fourth and is it turned out last, time. He then travelled across Spain and into southern France, where he is believed to have painted the delightful *Provencal Street Scene* now in the Eton College collection. From here he went to Genoa, onto Rome by June, and thence to his beloved Venice where amongst others, he painted a large oil of the *Piazetta of St. Marks* which went into private hands. This was unusually early in the year for James to be in Venice, since he preferred the more effective lighting conditions of early autumn. Unfortunately, on his return to England, he found yet more health troubles had descended on the family.

The last surviving child from his marriage, Emma Lavinia, who had stuck with her father through thick and thin, was decidedly poorly. She had never been very strong, and had long suffered from bronchial disorders, which had now become much worse. Dr Fuller was called in and gave a gloomy prognosis. Indeed, Emma failed to show any signs of recovery throughout the spring and early summer of 1860 as had been hoped, and she then developed lung congestion, finally passing away on 16 July, just five weeks short of her birthday. James was present at the end, and registered the death himself, although curiously he gave her age as 37, when she was actually still 36. By this time, most of the central London cemeteries were full, and in 1839 following the passing in Parliament of the Burial Act four years previously, a vast new one had been opened by the London Cemetery Company at Swains Lane, Highgate in the northern suburbs. On Holland's behalf, Dr Fuller purchased a grave there for the sum of six guineas.

James went to Venice as usual that autumn, but does not seem to have had much enthusiasm for his work. He began a work entitled *Waiting for our Gondola, Murano,* but it was not to be finished until some three years later, and it was still in the studio when he died. The title is interesting; who does he refer to by "our"? Had Charlotte travelled to Venice with him, or was it another of his artist friends? He did complete a water-colour study of the *Doge's Palace and the Dogana* during this visit.

The house in Osnaburgh Street must have still seemed strange when he returned, consisting as far as we know of the middle-aged and rather sickly Mary Morrant, his two daughters by Charlotte - who were by now using his surname - and a Scottish girl servant. Charlotte herself may not have been a permanent resident, certainly she is not listed in the 1861 census. Perhaps she was spending time looking after her 73 year old mother, or maybe there was ill-feeling between herself and her older sister Mary, who had run Holland's house for so very many years. More likely though is the suggestion that yet another young lady had entered the artist's life, one Emily West, a petite and attractive 17 year old blonde.

Her father William West, was a baker, who had suffered more than his fair share of both matrimonial troubles and extramarital liaisons, resulting in four daughters, all of whom shared his house in St. Pancras. They became well known amongst the artist fraternity, as West supplemented his meagre income by offering them as *"models set to artists."* They were all for hire by the time they were seven and seemingly in great demand. Holland had used Emily as a model on occasion for several years, but around 1860 or 1861 this appears to have developed into something more than a professional relationship. Certainly his showing at the Water-colour Society's 1861 exhibition of an unremarkable single work, indicates that his mind may have been elsewhere; the British Institution received a pair of oils. Furthermore, he failed to travel abroad that autumn, although he did some painting on the south coast, including ***Eastbourne,*** finished off a large ***Venice*** oil, and on 29 October painted Emily West in his studio. This work, entitled ***Portrait of a Woman in Blue,*** carries both Holland's monogram and the initials E.W., and today rests in the British Museum.

It seems that Charlotte, not unreasonably, took strong exception to this new woman in Holland's life. She was by now 44 and had had two children by a man who, for reasons that can only be guessed, would not marry her. Now he seemed to be infatuated with a girl four years younger than his eldest surviving daughter Louisa, who had just come of age. Charlotte decided to act, and took her daughters away to live with her at 10 Orchard Street, Kentish Town, where they resumed the use of the Morrant surname. Young Alice would have had no say in the matter, but how readily Louisa agreed to go can only be guessed at, not least because she was being taken away from an affluent lifestyle to something considerably more modest and down to earth. She was also extremely fond of her father, but as matters turned out, the move was to have a profound effect on her future. A young man by the name of Arthur John Hird was about to come into her life.

Arthur was the son of a notable West End solicitor Charles Hird and his wife Mary, and by

Oxford Street (*The Queen's London*)

1851 he was a draper's assistant in his cousin and step-brother Henry Samuel's business at 363 Oxford Street; he was just 26 years old. By 1862, Arthur was a hosier with his own business at 76 High Street, Camden Town, then a good middle class residential area. This was close to where Charlotte and her children were living after the split with Holland, and it was not long before Louisa called into Hird's shop to make a purchase, a chance meeting which was to develop into friendship and then romance. Tradition has it that no news of this relationship filtered back to Holland until Arthur Hird, at Charlotte's instigation, called upon him to ask for his daughters hand in marriage. This was late in 1861 or early in 1862, and

Greenwich Hospital (The Queen's London)

The Greenwich Railway

it seems to have had quite an effect on James. Perhaps it brought home to him the parental responsibilities he still had, and how foolish he had been, but the upshot was that shortly after this meeting he ended his relationship with Emily West, who moved back to 15 Grafton Street.

He now seemed to find renewed vigour in his painting, returning to many of his old haunts, including Greenwich. Here he painted an oil of the steps of the Hospital's famous Painted Hall, which had been designed by Christopher Wren as a refectory and since 1823 had been used as an art gallery. That summer he returned to the Water-colour Society in far more typical vein, with six works on show; four Venetians, one of Rotterdam and one of roses. The Art Journal was moved to write that the Rotterdam picture was "a broad, honest daylight drawing." Strangely, for the first time in over thirty years, he failed to exhibit at the British Institution, but had two works on show at the 1862 International Exhibition, *The Rialto, Venice* and *St. Laurence, Rotterdam - an October Morning.* That autumn he returned to Venice, where he painted an oil of the *Doge's Palace* for Louis Huth of Possingworth Manor, Waldron, Sussex. Huth was a cousin of Charles Huth of

Oakhurst, Tunbridge Wells, who was himself a keen collector of Holland's work.

Upon his return from the Continent, he summoned Arthur Hird once again, to explain to him the circumstances of Louisa's birth. Arthur apparently took the news in good humour, enquiring whether he would be marrying a Miss Holland or a Miss Morrant! James gave his consent for the marriage and told Arthur that, if the advice of his lawyers (Parker Lambert and Durrant of 45 Pall Mall) was favourable, he would prefer that Louisa go to the church as Miss Holland.

That matter satisfactorily resolved, Holland busied himself with preparing his exhibition entries for 1863. He was in the British Institution with two oils, and the Water-colour Society with four works. The Art Journal praised his **Rialto** and his *"rapturous love of colour."* The picture was bought, before the exhibition opened, by Birkett Foster, who was on the hanging selection committee, and who later told a friend that he thought it was one of the finest works Holland had ever done. He had gone up to Osnaburgh Street and completed the purchase the very evening of the day that he first saw it.

The wedding was now fast approaching, and seeing to all the arrangements brought James and Charlotte back together for a time, although Alice seems to have stayed at Charlotte's home. The ceremony took place on 30th May 1863 at nearby St.Pancras parish church, the same church where at least two of Holland's sons had been baptised all those years ago. The witnesses were two of Arthur's cousins, while his father, by then a widower, was too ill to attend and in fact died two months later. Louisa and Arthur went on honeymoon and James left for a painting journey around England, in the course of which he returned to Burslem for what was probably the last time. While in the area he painted some studies of *Keele Hall,* then the home of the Sneyd family.

That year saw the Water-colour Society start a series of winter exhibitions of sketches, and Holland made a sterling effort to support it. He had no fewer than fourteen frames containing a total of 35 sketches on show and, no doubt well satisfied, set off for a late visit to Venice. As had so often been the case, while he was away, family circumstances moved on and when he returned, it was to receive the delightful news that Louisa was pregnant with his first grandchild.

However, this great joy was tempered by the knowledge that the ever faithful Mary Morrant, who had suffered with bronchitis for years, was declining at an alarming rate; in fact Holland was about to be dealt a double blow. She developed tubercular pneumonia just after Christmas and died in the house at Osnaburgh Street on 26 January at the age of 53. James had Emma's grave at Highgate opened up, and Mary interred with his daughter, a mark of his great affection for her.

Just two weeks later came the second major shock. James's long and dear friend William Henry Hunt - whom he now called Old Billy - also died. Against his doctor's advice, he had gone to the Water-colour Society to review works by new artists seeking election and had caught a bad cold which ended in apoplexy. Once again, Holland took the sad journey to Highgate and must have begun to muse on his own mortality. He was now 64, comfortably off, but with a host of family entanglements that would need to be set straight in his affairs before too long; it was time to make his will.

CHAPTER SEVEN
THE TWILIGHT YEARS

Directly after Old Billy Hunt's funeral, James Holland called on his solicitor George Durrant in his offices at 23 Guildford Street, Russell Square, and asked him to draw up his will. The resulting eight page document was signed on 10 March, with George Durrant and his clerk Ambrose Cudden acting as witnesses. Charlotte and her daughters were the main beneficiaries, and were described as living at 10 Orchard Street, Kentish Town. On each of the following two days a codicil was added, the first bequeathing to *"Emily Hart (commonly called West)"* the sum of one hundred guineas *"in order to mark my sense of her good conduct during many years."* At that time Emily was still unmarried and living with her parents. The second codicil, which was signed by Ambrose Cudden and Charles Dudman, benefited George Durrant himself, who was to be left *"the antique intaglio gold ring which I usually wear as a token of my regard."*

That duty out of the way, Holland prepared six Venetian works for the Water-colour Society exhibition, including **Waiting for Our Gondola** which he had begun in 1860 just after Emma's death. The Art Journal review was low key, and he failed to get into the British Institution that summer. As far as his domestic circumstances were concerned, he had filled the void left by Mary's death by taking in her 39 year old sister Sarah as his new housekeeper. One of Louisa Hird's daughters would in later years describe Sarah as a *"kind of servant to grandmother Holland"* and she had become known in the family as "Hty", which is how Alice had tried to say "Auntie."

Thus it seems almost certain that at about this time, notwithstanding the address given in Holland's will, Charlotte too was once more back under his roof, together with the 14 year old Alice; Louisa's marriage and the impending arrival of the first grandchild must have smoothed over much of the previous rancour between them. Certainly in the last years of her long life Charlotte was known as Mrs Holland. Then on 10 May Louisa gave birth to a healthy baby girl, who was to be baptised Amy Louisa and would herself grow to become a gifted amateur artist.

After a trip to Greenwich during which he painted the hospital yet again, James left for Venice in the autumn, but it seems he did not take Charlotte with him, since a friend of hers during the last twenty years of her life never heard her speak of travelling on the Continent. Perhaps during that winter, he undertook what was presumably a commission, by producing a water-colour entitled **The Burning of HMS Bombay**. On 14 December 1864, HMS Bombay, a 2nd rate 67 gun vessel, mysteriously caught fire near Flores Island in the estuary of the River Plate in South America, whilst preparing to take part in target practice. Out of a crew of 616, eighty six perished in the disaster.

Holland's six entries in the 1865 Water-colour Society exhibition were all Venetians, but this was to be the last year in which his work was specifically mentioned by the Art Journal which said that his *"highly coloured Venetian scenes"* were largely *"products for effect"*. It also singled out his **Riva Degli Schiavoni** saying *"this drawing is not wholly satisfactory: its multitudinous materials are* *scattered and the lights, darks and colour want focused force."* Such a negative notice would have been of little consequence to Holland now; apart from his advancing age and comfortable circumstances, his non-exhibition work was still in great demand.

Louisa was expecting her second child that summer, but James left for Venice as usual before it was born. Although he probably did not know it then, this was to be his last visit to the city he loved so much and one of the water-colours he finished, *Santa Maria Della Salute with Gondola,* can be seen in Preston's Harris Art Gallery. He had been coming to Venice for thirty years, through the early privations of packhorse and carriage to the more relaxed steamer and railway era, and must have become a familiar figure amongst the great number of artists who were drawn to this wonderful city. In fact, not only was he destined never again to return here, but he would not undertake another painting expedition anywhere in the time he had left. Many of his contemporaries were falling by the wayside. Hunt was gone, Joshua Cristell from the Longport days had lived near him in Osnaburgh Street for two years but was now dead, as were other artist neighbours such as Frederick Mackenzie and George Lance.

Louisa's baby arrived on 22 September; it was a boy, but as James was still away, he was not baptised until the first month of the new year, when he was named James Henry Arthur Hird at St. Pancras parish church. Perhaps the first two names were chosen in remembrance of James's own son who had had such a tragically short life almost forty years before. More likely though, it was that having chosen James for obvious reasons, Henry came from Arthur Hird's uncle Henry Samuel, who was one of the child's god parents.

Holland now settled into a quiet and relaxed lifestyle. He was a great conversationalist, enjoying the company of an extensive circle of friends who would come to Osnaburgh Street and chatter for hours on end. A letter to an acquaintance survives in Camden Library:

"Dear Tomkins, A dozen of our mutual friends 'members of The Club' have promised to meet in my Den for a gossip on Tuesday next the 19th inst at 8 of the clock. Need I say that I most especially desire the pleasure of your company on that occasion. I am ever most faithfully yours, James Holland."

On 5 November 1866, his third grandchild arrived and was called Frederick Charles after an uncle. It seems likely that the services of the long-standing family doctor Charles Chinner Fuller were called on once

The first page of James Holland's will, drawn up in 1864.

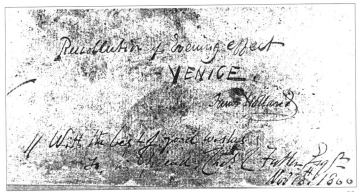

more to attend the birth, since just two weeks later, James gave him a water-colour *Recollections of Evening Effect Venice*, inscribed on the reverse after the artist's signature - *"With the best of good wishes to his friend Charles C. Fuller Esquire. Nov 18th 1866."*

Regrettably however, despite the rejoicing for the new arrival, all was not well financially with Arthur Hird, who moved again during the year to 156 High Street, Camden Town. By 1869 he had become an employee rather than an employer, and it seems that his brother, his father-in-law and Herbert Samuel may have rallied round to bail him out

Holland still busied himself from time to time with the affairs of the Water-colour Society. In particular, he took on much of the burden of organising the winter exhibitions of sketches, which were aimed at attracting unfinished works in pencil, chalk or colours. With his good friends Frederick Burton and John Gilbert, both of whom had been instrumental in persuading him to stand for re-election to the Society in 1856, Holland formed the hanging committee. He was by far the oldest of the three; Gilbert was born in Greenwich in 1817 and may have been a pupil of James's when they both lived in that area. He was elected President of the Water-colour Society the year after Holland died and was then knighted before becoming an Associate of the Royal Academy in 1872 and a full member in 1876. Frederick Burton was an Irishman born in 1816; he became director of the National Gallery in 1874, was also later knighted and died in 1900.

In these final years, Holland was also on the selection committee for the main spring exhibition and in 1866 performed an act of great kindness to help a younger artist. Frederick Shields had intended offering a work entitled The Bread Watch, but because of ill health, delivered it to the Society well after the entry date, with the exhibition already selected and hung. James however, was so impressed with the work, that he took one of his own off the wall and replaced it with Shield's water-colour.

In both 1865 and 1866 Holland had six works in the Water-colour Society exhibitions, but was absent from the British Institution. He was now producing rather less work, for in 1867 his Water-colour Society entry dropped to three. However, he returned to the British Institution with four oils, for his last showing with them, since the lease on their gallery had expired. Apparently a brief painting trip into the West Midlands was undertaken that year, for amongst others he completed a water-colour entitled *The Kingfisher's Haunt, Lord Leigh's Park, Worcestershire*. The following year the Water-colour Society had just two works in the spring, but James maintained his average of ten frames at the winter sketches exhibition.

With the opening of 1869, Holland's final exhibiting year had arrived and he seemed to be back to something like his previous form. He had five water-colours in the spring exhibition, the most interesting of which was a return to his flower painting roots with **Study of Roses in my Garden at Blackheath, 1839.** Why had this work surfaced again after so many years? It seems likely that this was an act of pure nostalgia on the artist's part, looking back with great affection to happy times with Charlotte. Perhaps too, he was well aware that this might be one of his last exhibitions, for by the time it opened he was far from well and was gradually becoming more and more housebound.

Dr Fuller who was by then becoming one of the foremost surgeons of his day, still attended to his dear friend, but it would

The older James Holland. Photograph 1860s.

seem there was little to be done to halt the steady decline of a man now in his 71st year. James made one last effort for the Water-colour Society winter exhibition, submitting no fewer than 14 sketches, including one of Greenwich and two done on one of the Welsh journeys with Charlotte. Most poignant of all was the last sketch, entitled simply **Market Over** - he must have known.

On 3 February, Louisa had her fourth child, Isabella Alice, but it is unlikely that James ever saw her. The Water-colour Society exhibition was still on the walls in the Pall Mall gallery when the end finally came on Sunday 13 February 1870. James failed to awaken from a long night's sleep and Dr Fuller arrived to certify him dead from *"cirrhosis of the liver and exhaustion"* - the pleasures of an affluent lifestyle coupled with advancing age. Sarah Morrant went to register the death, and strangely entered the date as 12 February, although the sworn probate and the grave give it as the 13th. On the following Wednesday, The Times published a notice of the death which simply read *"On the 12th Feb at No.8 Osnaburgh Street, Regent's Park, James Holland Esq. of the Society of Painters in Water-Colours."*

The next day the Daily News also announced the death and the Illustrated London News followed suit on the 19th saying:

"Mr. James Holland, the well-known member of the Society of Painters in Water-colours, died on the 12th inst. In the early part of his career Mr.Holland practised as a flower painter, which may account for his excellence as a colourist and the florid character of his colouring, especially in his later works. In middle life Mr. Holland painted much in oil, with a success that renders it somewhat surprising that he did not continue to work

in that medium. Whether painting in oil or water-colour Mr. Holland drew nearly the whole of his subjects, after quitting flower-painting, from Venice."

There was a lengthy and glowing obituary in The Athenaeum on 19 February, which commented on his ***Study of Roses in My Garden at Blackheath***, **1839** water-colour, exhibited the previous year at the Water-colour Society; *"Looking at this example of what was done in that art a generation since, was no unprofitable exercise for one's humility; it was an invaluable lesson for the current school."* The obituary went on to say *"His reputation grew with practice and the passing of time"* and that his illustrations for annuals were done *"in a manner and with results the exquisite delicacy and poetry of which are well known to all who have seen those gems of his pencil."*

They also made a quite scathing criticism of the fact that the Royal Academy had never seen fit to elect Holland to their ranks; *"That such a painter as Mr Holland should not have been elected a member of the Royal Academy, which is popularly supposed to comprise the most worthy in the profession, was a mystery to all who were not well informed. That the Academy should have been content with such landscape painters as those whom it recently lost in the persons of Mr. Creswick and Mr. Witherington, when Mr. Linnell offered himself for thirty-one years and Mr. Holland was at hand, is another wonder."* A very similar notice appeared in the Art Journal the following month.

A few days after his death, a large number of artists, friends and relatives gathered at 8 Osnaburgh Street, and as was the custom, Charlotte, Alice and Sarah watched from the windows as the funeral cortege set off on its sad journey up to Highgate. The same grave that already held his daughter Emma and Mary Morrant was opened again, and James was laid to rest with them. For the next century or more, the gradual decay that beset Highgate cemetery would see the artist's memorial fall into a sad state of neglect and disrepair, until it was restored by the family in 1994.

CHAPTER EIGHT
THE FAMILY LEFT BEHIND

James Holland's will was proved on 4 March 1870 on behalf of Sawbridge and Wrentmore of 126 Wood Street, Cheapside, being sworn at the under £5,000 level for probate duty. A notice for creditors to contact them was published in the London Gazette. His executors were named as his bank manager Henry Cundell of 4 Stratford Place, who renounced probate, leaving matters in the hands of the second executor, the good Dr Fuller. George Durrant, the solicitor who had drawn up the will, had himself passed away at the age of 48 some four months previously and so who attended to read it to the family is not known.

Holland had directed that *"all my pictures, sketches, studies and other artistic property and effects"* were to be disposed of *"by public auction at the office of Messieurs Christie Manson and Company."* The residue of his estate after funeral expenses, etc, was to be invested in public funds or government securities as the executors saw fit. From the annual interest on these investments, Charlotte was to receive £80 *"for her separate use until Alice Morrant (whom I hereinafter call Alice Holland and whom I desire to be hereinafter known by that name) shall attain the age of twenty one years or marry with such consent"* (of her guardian). Thereafter, Charlotte would receive £100 a year for the rest of her life - a tidy sum in those days - and in addition she was left all his furniture, linen, china, plate, wines and other household goods, plus a further £50 to be paid to her within 30 days of his death to see to her mourning expenses. The balance of the income from the estate was to be divided equally between Alice and Louisa, but a careful clause ensured that neither Louisa's husband, nor Alice's if she were to marry, would have access to the income in the event of their being declared bankrupt.

The oils, water-colours and sketches left in James's studio after his death were duly auctioned by Christie's as directed between Thursday 26th and Saturday 28th May. The catalogue described the sale as *"comprising about fifty pictures and sketches in oils including several important works which were exhibited at the Royal Academy, and upwards of four hundred beautiful drawings and sketches in water-colours and pencil, made in Italy, Venice, Portugal, France, England and Wales, also a few pictures and drawings by other artists, engravings, artistic accessories, costumes, etc., etc."*

The sale commenced at 1 o'clock on the Thursday, with a total of 518 pictures being sold. The first day realised the sum of £1,322, the second £69 and the third £1,110 for a grand total of £2,501, which necessitated the estate being re-sworn at the under £6,000 mark - a good amount for those days. Dr Fuller attended the sale and paid one guinea for four drawings of views in Switzerland, over £13 each for water-colours of a canal scene in Rotterdam and a Welsh waterfall, 26/- for **Notre Dame Rouen**, and nearly £9 for a **Dordrecht** water-colour. A member of the Hird family paid one guinea for a Folkestone beach scene sketch.

With the artist's affairs settled, Charlotte, Alice and Sarah immediately left Osnaburgh Street for the last time and went to live with Charlotte's mother at Stewart's Grove Tottenham. The old lady was 84 however, and to add to the family's grief she suffered a severe bout of summer colic and died in Alice's arms before July was out. For the fourth and final time, the grave at Highgate was opened on the instructions of Dr Fuller to receive her. Charlotte and the others now had to move again, and they took themselves off to live quietly at 7 Birbeck Road Islington, where they were residing by the time of the 1881 census, with Charlotte being known as Mrs Holland. They later uprooted yet again to Lawn Terrace, Holloway until Sarah died of cancer on 31 May 1885 at the age of 60. In her last days she was attended yet again by Dr Charles Fuller, who had probably promised James that he would look after the ladies for as long as he was able. He was still living in Albany Street, although he had moved to number 33 by this time, and had a practice at St. Andrews Place.

Soon after Sarah's death, Charlotte and Alice moved to 20 Fenwick Road just off the East Dulwich Road in Peckham, South London, and in the 1891 census are listed as *"living on their own means"*. Here they met the Reverend Frank Mills Smith, a powerfully persuasive Baptist preacher who had built a church in the area and who lived in the East Dulwich Road with his wife and young family. The house has long since been demolished, with the site now being covered by a block of flats. Mrs Joyce Smith died in January 1892, and Charlotte and Alice were among those who offered to help look after the Rev. Smith's children whenever he was away preaching. Alice and Frank subsequently fell in love, and were married at the Peckham Rye Tabernacle on 2 May 1893, the redoubtable Dr Fuller giving her away and signing the register as a witness together with his wife. Charlotte went to live with the newly-weds.

After just four years of marriage, Alice became ill and on consulting her doctor was told that she had developed cancer of the liver. She immediately made her will leaving everything to her husband and died on 16 July 1898 with him beside her, being buried alongside Frank's first wife Joyce in the same grave in Forest Hill cemetery. Charlotte remained with Frank in his home at 21 Tyrwhitt Road, Lewisham and later still with his third wife at 11 Boveney Road, Honor Oak Park. She had her own rooms, furnished with items that she had brought from Osnaburgh Street and still had her income from James's estate.

In May 1905 Charlotte made a will, describing herself as *"Charlotte Martha Holland, widow of James Holland, artist."* She divided all her remaining money between Louisa and Frank and bequeathed a gold chain given to her by James, to Louisa's daughter "Flossie" (Florence) Bond, the author's grandmother, who was born four years after Holland's death. Charlotte also left a watch to May Hird, Louisa's seventh child, and to her youngest, Guy, *"three pencil cases, one gold and two silver, and a few useful things which his mother will find in one of my corner drawers."* She left her clothes equally between Louisa and her sister Emma Rachel. To Frank she left *"one double chest of drawers, one easy chair, one writing table, one sofa, one bedstead and mattress, one bolster, two pillows and any blankets that may be on my bed"* plus *"My dear Alice's gold watch and a parcel of silver which will be found in my small tin box with his name on it."* Many of these items obviously held fond memories of James for her and provided a source of comfort in her last few years.

Charlotte died at the grand old age of 92 on 12 August 1909, and her will was sworn at a modest £279. She was buried in Frank's family plot at Forest Hill; how sad that the whole width of London separated her from the final resting place of the only love in her life. She took with her to the grave the secret of why they never married. Frank Smith was to live on to the age of 83 and marry for a fourth time before passing peacefully away in 1930 and joining his first two wives and Charlotte in Forest Hill. Despite recent tidying up in the cemetery, which has seen many headstones cleared away, the impressive Smith memorial remains in place.

Of all the people who had been closest to Holland, now only his daughter Louisa remained and she had certainly found her later married life trying. Altogether she had had eight children by her husband Arthur, although her fourth, Isobel Alice, the daughter born just days before James's death, only lived for eight years. (She too is buried at Highgate, but in a different grave). The fifth child was another son born on 15 August 1871 and named Holland Hird in honour of his grandfather, while number six was Florence Mary, born on 17 February 1874. Then came May Johnston on 28 February 1879 and last of all, Guy Cecil two days before Christmas in 1883.

In 1869 Arthur's hosiery business in Camden Town fell on hard times as the area deteriorated, and certainly by 1871, he had become a perfumier's clerk, then a clerk in H.M. Office of Works later that same year. Arthur ended his working life as a commercial traveller with the firm of Hird and Inglis, Woollen Merchants, 30 Newgate Street, London EC. The business had been founded by Henry Hird and was by this time run by two of Arthur's own sons, Holland and James. All this turmoil was reflected in constant moving of the family home, with the Hirds progressing from Camden Town to Nightingale Road Edmonton, and 84 Kings Road Southsea, where he worked as a fancy draper for Joseph Dyer. In the 1891 census he is at 11 Fenwick Road, East Dulwich, just a few doors away from Charlotte and Alice, and is still described as a commercial traveller.

Arthur died at the age of 70 on 9 February 1901 at home, without leaving a will - he probably had nothing to leave - and was buried at Forest Hill cemetery, not far from the Smith family plot. Later that same year, Arthur's 84 year old brother also died, and left the sum of £50 to Louisa and each of her children, which must have been welcome indeed as she appears to have used her share of the income from James's invested estate to support Arthur in his failed business ventures. This would of necessity have been with the approval of the trustee Dr Fuller, who after gathering numerous medical honours in his long career, died in 1902.

Louisa went on to spend the last few years of her life with her daughter Florence, who knew her as Grandma Holland, and who was now married to Percy William Bond, at 51 Overhill Road, Dulwich. Just a few months after Charlotte's death, Louisa made her will, a document marking the point from which many family treasures from the Osnaburgh Street days began to disappear into obscurity. To her eldest daughter Amy Reynolds, by then a widow living in Horsham, she left a gold ring, Charlotte's wedding ring and a photograph of James Holland, but none of these items stayed in the Reynolds family. Amongst a variety of trinkets left to Florence were three of particular interest; the miniature of James's daughter Elizabeth which had helped to preserve for Louisa such fond memories of her "auntie", one of his flower paintings and a mourning ring. This ring could have been associated with Holland's wife, one of his daughters, or indeed could even have been Charlotte's mourning ring for him. Regrettably, both this and the miniature were subsequently stolen from Florence's home by burglars.

May, who would be the last survivor of the grandchildren, passing away in 1913, was also left a Holland flower picture, while Guy received yet more pictures plus several small items including a card case that was probably James's and a gold locket that had once belonged to Elizabeth Anne. It was a great tribute to Louisa that, despite her difficult family circumstances, she had somehow managed to keep all these reminders of Osnaburgh Street together throughout her life; she must have loved her father very deeply. The other three sons were not mentioned in the will; James Henry had emigrated to the United States in the early 1900s and Holland had gone to Canada a few years earlier - both today have large families of descendants in those countries. Frederick Charles although married in 1889 and having a son who lived until 1975 and a daughter, had disappeared from the scene.

Louisa died at Overhill Road on 26 May 1913 at the age of 73, being buried with her husband at Forest Hill; the grave now lost in dense undergrowth. Although her son James Henry, who was four when the artist died and could just conceivably have remembered him, lived until 1947, effectively Louisa's passing severed the last direct connection with James. For the next 70 years most of the surviving descendants and their offspring would allow James to slip quietly into the mists of the past and obscurity.

A young James sketched by his friend William Henry ('Bird's Nest') Hunt.

CHAPTER NINE
REDISCOVERY

In the years following Holland's death, despite his absence from public exhibitions, recognition of his talent continued among his many collectors. The Athenaeum carried a series entitled *Visits to Private Galleries*, and in the year of his death, reviewed two of James's works in the collection of Frederick Craven, Esq., Hope Lodge, Manchester. *The Entrance to the Grand Canal, Venice* was described as being *"one of the brightest versions of Venice that have perhaps ever been painted; it is everywhere an unbroken breadth of daylight, uninterrupted sunshine, with evidences rather of pleasure than of business, and just movement enough to rescue the place from the supposition of its being a region of dreamland. At least a hundred times have we seen these same objects painted, but never any local representation so daring and defiant, yet so profoundly argumentative. Everything in Venice refers us to the past, and thus Mr. Holland paints the place as it was - the pearl of the Adriatic, for there is enough of the visionary in the drawing to tell us that it is historical and of yesterday, rather than the real and of today. Few men have ever been sufficiently interested in the narrow canals to paint them, yet Holland has studied them and rendered them, both in oil and water-colour, with magical effect."* The second Holland in the collection was *The Lion of St. Mark*.

From time to time throughout the remainder of the 19th century and on into the 20th, Holland's were seen in temporary exhibitions, or would appear from private collections as bequests to major galleries. The Manchester Royal Jubilee Exhibition of 1887 displayed a large Venetian oil which was part of the collection of one Stephen G. Holland (no relation), bought at the 1870 sale of the artist's effects. The Royal Academy Exhibition of British Art in 1934 included a view of the *Piazza of St.Mark's*.

Other works cropped up in the London auction houses, where they realised wildly fluctuating prices depending on whether or not the Victorian era was fashionable at that time. Shortly before the 1st World War, Holland's were selling for very high prices indeed, before falling away dramatically throughout the 1920s, 30s and 40s, picking up again in the early 1960s. Essentially however, he remained just another artist, overshadowed by the better known names of the period.

In the late 1960s the Bond family of High Wycombe in Buckinghamshire, who were descended from James Holland via his grand-daughter Florence, unexpectedly received a draft manuscript of a proposed biography of the artist, from a newspaper proprietor in Shropshire. The author was Morley Tonkin, who had somehow become fascinated by Holland and having tracked down this surviving arm of the family, asked for the Bonds' help with details of the personal life of both James and those who followed him. Florence's son Cyril Bond had married Rose Allen in 1933, and by a remarkable coincidence, she also displayed considerable talent as an artist in both oils and water-colour, and had become a Royal Academy exhibitor just a few years before the contact with Morley Tonkin.

Up until that time, the family new little about Holland, beyond that they were related to him, and the manuscript aroused considerable interest for a time, with two Holland oils being acquired via London dealers. Tonkin had also been in touch with the Hird descendants in Canada, but the two arms of the family were more or less unaware of each other. Almost another twenty years were to pass before the manuscript was picked up and studied in earnest once again, this time by the Bond's son - the author - and his wife Christine. We read the story properly for the first time and were fired with enthusiasm to discover all we could about the life and work of this neglected artist. In this quest we were joined by my elder sister Janet, for whom genealogical research had been a way of life for very many years.

We quickly discovered that in the intervening years since Morley Tonkin had been at work, much had happened to make our work considerably more difficult, not least the sad discovery that Tonkin himself had passed away, and that his extensive notes had not survived. His manuscript had been published in a very much abridged form in the journal of the Old Water-colour Society in 1966, but surviving letters showed that he had continued his research for some time after this - how much he could probably have told us! It was also found when we began following the artist's trail around London, that some of his haunts had changed out of all recognition since Tonkin had visited them, with several houses, most notably the one in Greenwich, demolished and re-developed beyond all recognition.

The last significant discovery in these early days was that regrettably, much of Tonkin's work was flawed, with several important threads of James's personal life story being either incomplete or simply incorrect. At this stage, we were just enjoying tracking down Holland's work in various galleries and collections, and his family in parish records, but two things happened to change the course of our work and lead to this biography.

In the summer of 1985, we decided to visit his grave at Highgate and after a telephone call to make an appointment, arrived at the imposing gates of the London Cemetery on a dank and overcast day in July. We were ushered into a small room were the large and musty burial ledgers were stored, but were told that no trace of a James Holland could be found! Initially dismayed, we asked to look through the pages for 1870 ourselves, just in case, and to our immense relief, there he was. We were then guided to the general area of the grave, which was considerably overgrown, as the Friends of Highgate had yet to start their admirable work of tidying the cemetery. With not a little trouble, James's last resting place was finally found, neglected for over a century, with the headstone inscriptions barely discernible. Standing in that eerie and atmospheric place, looking at the sad memorial, with the rain dripping off the overhanging trees onto our umbrellas, we both instantly knew there was no stopping there. We simply had to find out all we could about this man who the rest of the world seemed to have forgotten.

Then in 1987 we saw for the first time, the magnificent collection of Holland water-colours so carefully stored away in the vaults of the Victoria and Albert Museum in South Kensington. It was a sunny day, and as the light streamed into the viewing room we lifted each picture gently out of the storage boxes to marvel in stunned silence at the delicate hand and brilliance of colour which met our eyes. They were so fresh that it was as if the artist had only just put down his brushes and stepped away for a break from his toil. This revelation spurred us on to see more, until we finally came to the excellent art gallery and museum in Stoke-on-Trent. Here we discovered not only many more superb works, but an enthusiastic pride in their local artist, which had lead them to mount a Holland exhibition in

1970. We found there was ready agreement that perhaps something should be done again for the bicentenery of his birth, in 1999 - and would it not be a good idea if his life could be properly chronicled at the same time? With renewed energy, and encouraged by the many Holland enthusiasts we encountered at art galleries up and down the country, we set out on the long road to discover not only the artist, but just exactly who the man was behind these wonderful pictures.

The next surprise came when we started cataloguing his work, and discovered just how prolific an artist he had been. Almost every major art gallery and museum in the United Kingdom, plus a considerable number overseas, answered our enquiries positively - yes they had Hollands in their collections, in some cases considerable quantities of them! Visits to the leading London auction houses also showed that James's work regularly cropped up in their sales, passing from one private owner to another, and careful study of their catalogues revealed the existence of many more pictures than had previously been identified by us, or which had been listed in the Tonkin manuscript. No doubt many of these were originally painted for patrons rather than for public exhibition and sale. How many more must there be, just waiting to be unearthed? We found a London art dealer who was a great fan of Holland's work, and who not only regularly had a selection in his gallery, but who had also sold something like ninety over a two year period. One painting in particular still eludes us, the 1853 oil **Nellie Nick**, James's portrait of his lover Charlotte, which was known to be in a private collection in the 1960s.

Since the Second World War, the pattern of occasional public appearances by Holland works has continued. In May 1949 The Illustrated London News reproduced his 1850 **View of Charing Cross** which now resides in the Huntington Library in California. The same collection's water-colour of **Walmer Castle** was shown in a 1955 Arts Council exhibition of the Gilbert Davis collection, which included a large number of Holland's and to which it at that time belonged. In 1956 Colnaghi's showed an 1850 **Rouen** water-colour in their *Water Colours of Three Centuries Exhibition.* As recently as 1990, the Bankside Gallery in London showed several Holland's in their Visions of Venice exhibition, while a year earlier the Victoria and Albert Museum saw fit to use the 1844 Venetian study, **Hospital of the Pieta** as one of the illustrations for that year's calendar.

These are rare glimpses however, for the delicate nature of water-colours in particular, dictates that they largely remain locked away and protected from the harmful effects of lengthy exposure to daylight and polluted air. The auction houses continue to offer the best chance of glimpsing - albeit briefly - one of James's works in all its glory. So far, the highest known price paid for a Holland at auction is £31,000 for his 1841 commission of **The Langford Family in their Drawing Room**, sold at Sotheby's in July 1989, while many of his less imposing works, such as the early flower studies, can today still be picked up for a few hundred pounds a time.

Almost two centuries have now passed since James Holland made his entrance into the world. In his seventy years he took many bold steps to further his chosen artistic career, and despite all the personal tragedy and turmoil that life threw at him, emerged with a proud and justified reputation for a remarkable talent. Perhaps one day this will receive rather more of the recognition he so richly deserves.

APPENDIX A: JAMES HOLLAND CATALOGUE - BY TITLE WHERE KNOWN

The works are listed wherever possible by the artist's own title. Where this is not known, the geographical location or a description of the subject matter is used.

Details of the current owners are included only in the case of collections accessible by the public. O = oil, S = sketch, W = water-colour, * = works in the possession of the artist at the time of his death

Across the Lagoon. W
After Market, Venice. W *
Afternoon. W 1869
After the Storm. $24^{1/4}$" x 36" O.
Airolo Pass of the St.Gothard. W 1837
Ajuda Palace, The. W *
Alcobaco $11^{1/2}$" x $16^{5/8}$" W. 1 Aug 1837. * V & A,
Alcobaco and Batalha. W 1863
Alexandria Harbour. W 1851
Almada from Mrs Belem's, Lisboa. W Jun 1837.
Al Marda Lisbon. W. Walker Gallery, Liverpool.
Ampezzo, Austrian Tyrol. W *
D'Ampezzo in the Tyrol. $18^{7/8}$" x $9^{1/4}$" W 1858.
Ampitheatre at Verona. W. Dublin museum in 1913.
Ampitheatre at Verona. 11" x $8^{5/8}$" W. Huntington Library.
Ampitheatre, Verona, The. W x 2 *
Amsterdam. W c.1845. Harrow School.
Anglers by a Cottage on a River Bank. O Stoke City Art Gallery.
Anna, Leiria. W x 2 *
Anniversary Festival of Battle of Trafalgar $1^{1/4}$" x $37^{1/4}$" W. National Maritime Museum.
Antiques. 14" x 20" O c.1841.
Antiques. 29" x 39" O 1841.
Antiques. W 1842
Antwerp. $9^{1/4}$" x $6^{1/2}$" W July 1837. Huntington Library.
Arcade, Genoa. O 1861
Atheneum drawing room. 18" x 12" O 1836.
At The Steps of St.Marks Square Venice. $1^{1/2}$" x 17" W.
Balcony, The. W *
Bar of the Douro. S. Used in "Tourist in Portugal".
Barbarigo Palace, Venice. W 1847
Basilica, San Marco. O 1859
Batalha. S. Used in "Tourist in Portugal".
Batalha. W 1866
Batalha. W x 3 *
Batalha, East End. S. Used in "Tourist in Portugal".
Bathing Machines. Sep 1861 x 2
Bathing Machines at Eastbourne. 6" x $3^{7/8}$" SW 9 Sep 1861.
Bathing Machines below Cliff. W 1861
Beach at Deal, The. W *
Beach Scene. 10" x $4^{1/4}$" S. Huntington Library.
Beckenham Church Porch. 11" x 9" W 1830. National Art Gallery, Wellington, New Zealand.
Bedroom of Lady Betty Germain, Knole, The. O 1845. Sissinghurst Castle.
Belfry, The. $7^{1/4}$" x 7" W.
Sir Belkford's Alcobaco and Monastery of Batalha. W Jun 1837.
Bella Venezia. W 1861
Below the Swallow Falls, After Rain, N.Wales. W 1863 *
Benediction, The. W 1867
Billingsgate Market. $44^{1/4}$" x 30" O.
Blackheath? O Stoke City Art Gallery. P 1990.
Blackwall Reach from Charlton Fields Blackheath. O V & A
Boats. W 12 Oct 1851.
Boats, Venice. W 1 Oct 1857.
Boats, Venice. W 1866
Boats and Beach Scene. $9^{3/4}$" x $4^{1/2}$" S. Huntington Library.
Boats and figures by the steps of a temple. 4" x $6^{3/8}$" W.
Boats at a Quay, Venice. W *
Boats on the Lake of Geneva. W *
Boats on the Shore, S.Pier da arena. W *
Bouquet of Flowers. $10^{1/2}$" x $8^{3/4}$" W.
Breakwater, The. W Sep 1861.
Bridge of Sighs, The. W 1843.
Bridge over Canal, Venice. W. Laing Gallery Newcastle.
Broadstairs. $13^{7/8}$" x $9^{3/8}$" W.
In the Brown Gallery, Knole. O 1845. Sissinghurst Castle, Kent.
Brown Gallery, Knole, The. W *
Brown Study, A. W 1832
Browning's House, Venice. W 1864.

Brunecken, Tyrol. O 1861
Buildings and Figures, Rouen. W *
Bunch of Flowers. O 1830. Stoke City Art Gallery.
Burning of HMS Bombay 14.12. 1864, The. 20" x 13$^{1/2}$" W.
Cacti, Coimbra. W 19 Aug 1837
Calleoni Monument, The.
?? - Camp of the Duke of - . W. V&A P 1987.
Canal at the Hague, A. W *
Canal at Venice with Ladies. 19$^{5/8}$" x 13$^{3/4}$" W. V & A
Canal Boats, Delft. W *
Canal in Venice. 15$^{5/8}$" x 9$^{5/8}$" W. V & A
Canal in Venice. 1845.
Canal Scene. O 1839
Canal Scene, Venice. O. Birmingham Art Gallery.
Canal Scene, Venice. W. Manchester Art Gallery.
Canal Scene, Venice. W x 10 *
Canal, Venice. O 1839
Cannoc Burn. Glen Affric, Loch Benevian. W 1858
Cantatrice, La. (With quotation). W 1864
Carnations. 7$^{1/2}$" x 10$^{1/2}$" W. V & A
Cartoon Gallery, Knole, The 865
Cathedral of St.Denis, Paris. 8$^{3/4}$" x 5$^{7/8}$" W 1831.
Cathedral of Dort on the River Maas, The
Cathedral, Genoa, The
Cathedral, Munich, The
Cathedral Tower, Antwerp. 10" x 5" W. V & A (Anon)
Catching the Pig at Boston Fair. O. Stoke City Art Gallery. (Holland attribution is suspect.)
Chapel of the Confessors, St.Marks. W. Laing Gallery Newcastle.
Chapel of the Penha. 11$^{3/4}$" x 17" W 1846. Huntington Library.
Chapel of the Pentra Convent, Cintra. W 1843
Chapel of St.John the Baptist in the Church of St.Roque, Lisbon. 15$^{1/2}$" x 11$^{1/4}$" W23 June 1837. *
Chapel of St.John the Baptist, Lisbon. O 1867
Chapel Room, Knole, The. O 1849
Chapel Room, Knole, The. 12$^{1/2}$" x 6$^{3/4}$" W.
Charing Cross. W 1835
Charing Cross. 11$^{3/4}$" x 7$^{3/4}$" W 1850. Huntington Library.
Charlton House, Kent. W 1844. Greenwich Art Gallery & Museum.
Chisholm's Pass - Col. Inge's Shooting, Glen Affric, Inverness, The. W 1859
Church Door, Verona, A. W 1863
Church doorway. W. Leger Galleries.
Church doorway, Genoa, A. W *
Church Interior, Batalha Portugal. 1$^{5/16}$" x 10$^{1/8}$" W 1837. Fitzwilliam.
Church Interior, Mafra. 17" x 11$^{3/4}$" SW 1837. Huntington Library.
Church of Estrella, Lisbon. W *
Church of Gesnati. W 20 Sep 1857.
Church of the Redentore, Venice, The. W 1857. *
Church of San Francisco. S. Used in "Tourist in Portugal".
Church of San Francisco, Oporto. W 1 July 1837. *
Church of San Francisco, Oporto. 17" x 11$^{3/4}$" W 30 Aug 1837. V & A
Church of SS.Giovanni E. Paolo, Venice. 15$^{1/8}$" x 12" W 1863. V & A
Church of St.Job, Venice. W *
Church of St.Joseph, Lisbon. W *
Church of Santa Maria de la Salute, Venice. S 1835. Whitworth Gallery, Manchester.
Church of St.Simeone, Venice. W *
Church of St.Sulpice. 7$^{5/8}$" x 4$^{1/8}$" W 1830s.
Church of St.Vincent, Rouen. O 1851
Church of St.Vincent, Rouen. S. Leeds Art Gallery.
Church of St.Vincent, Rouen. W *
Church Portal, Lisbon. 15$^{3/4}$" x 11$^{1/2}$" W 1837. Boston Museum of Fine Arts
Cintra. W. Southampton Art Gallery.
Cintra. W x 3 *
Cintra. W 1837. * V & A
Cintra. 11" x 16$^{3/4}$" W. V & A
Cistercian Monastry, Alcobaca, The. 10$^{3/16}$" x 14$^{1/4}$" W 1837. Fitzwilliam
Cliffs of Dover. 6$^{1/2}$" x 9$^{3/4}$" W Aug 1846.
Clifton. W 1863
Clifton Baths, Margate. 10" x 5" W. British Museum.
Cloister of the Monastery, Alcobaco, The. W *
Cloisters, Doria Palace, Genoa. W *
Clouds. W
Clouds. W 13 Sep
Clouds at Sundown. W
Cloudy Day. W 7 Sep 1861.
Coast of Genoa. O 1860
Coast near Folkestone, The. W *
Coast near Genoa, The. W *
Coast of Portugal, Women Bathing. 11$^{1/8}$" x 16$^{7/8}$" W 1859. V & A

Coast Scene. W 1835
Coast Scene, A. W *
Coast Scene (Eastbourne). W 9 Sep 1861.
Coast Scene with Boats and Figures. W
Coast Scene with Buildings. W
Coast Scene with Figures. W Sep 1861
Coast Scene with Sailing Vessels. W 13 Sep 1949.
Coast View. O 1834
Coast View. O 1835
Coimbra. S. Used in "Tourist in Portugal".
Coimbra. $11^{5/8}$" x $16^{7/8}$" W 19 Aug 1837. V & A
Coimbra. W x 2 *
Coimbra from the South - Portugal. W 1867
Colonnade, Genoa, A. W 1851. *
College Gate, Rochester. W 1831
Colleoni's Monument. 29" x 24" O 1851. Municipal Museum, Dublin.
Composition of Flowers. O 1830
Composition of Fruit. O 1829
Confessor's Chapel, Westminster Abbey. $10^{1/4}$" x 7" SW 1834. Cecil Higgins Gallery, Bedford.
Confessor's Chapel, Westminster Abbey (x 2). O 1835
Confessor's Chapel, Westminster Abbey. W 1840.
Convent at Batalha, The. W x 3 *
Convent of Mafra, Estremadura Portugal. $5^{1/4}$" x $9^{5/8}$" W. Fitzwilliam.
Convento Da Serra. $11^{9/16}$" x $16^{11/16}$" W 1 Sep 1837. * V & A
Conway. $16^{7/16}$" x $11^{1/2}$" O. Toledo Museum of Art.
Conway. W 1855 *
Coombe Martin. W *
Corfu. $28^{3/4}$" x 19" O 1851.
Cortina D'Ampezzo, distant view of. $14^{3/4}$" x $20^{1/2}$" W.
Cork Convent, Cintra, At the. W 1839
Cottage, North Wales, A. $14^{1/8}$" x $20^{5/8}$" W 8 October 1855.
Cottage Interior in North Wales. $21^{1/8}$" x $14^{3/8}$" W 1855. *
Countrymen with a White Horse. O. Stoke City Art Gallery.
Courtyard in Genoa. W. Wakefield Art Gallery.
Courtyard of Hotel de Cluny, Paris. 16" x 10" W.
Courtyard of a Venetian Palace. W 1838
Courtyard of a Venetian Palace. 33" x $23^{1/2}$" O 1839.
Croix de Pierre, Rouen. S 28 Aug 18?
Crouch Oak, The. O 1855
Deal Beach. O 1854
Deal Beach. $5^{1/2}$" x $8^{1/4}$" W 1847.
Deal Beach. W. Leeds Art Gallery.
Deal Beach. W 12 Sep 1847.
Deal Beach and Pier. W *
Deal Pier. W x 2 *
Delft. W 4 Oct 1845 *
Delft. W *
Delft (near). $5^{1/4}$" x $7^{1/4}$" S 29 Oct 1845. Huntington Library.
Demolition Work at London Bridge. $17^{7/8}$" x $5^{5/8}$" W 28 Jan 1832. Museum of London.
Departure for the Isle of Cytheria, after Watteau, The. W *
Devil's Bridge, The. $8^{7/8}$" x $11^{1/2}$" W.
Devonshire Stream, A. W *
Devotion. W 1844
Dianthus. 7" x $9^{1/2}$" W 1829. Huntington Library.
Didst Ever See a Gondola? W 1862
Dogana and Salute Church, The - Venice/Study of Effect After Rain. 12" x $16^{1/2}$" O 1848.
Dogana, Venice, The. (x 22) W 1859 (2 *)
Dogana, Venice, The. 10" diameter O c.1850.
Dogana Da Mare Ossia Di Transito, Venice. W 1843
Doges' Palace, The. O 1859
Doges' Palace, The. 16" x 29" O 1862
Doge's Palace, The. $20^{1/2}$" x $12^{1/4}$" W. Eton College.
Door of the Church of St.Lawrence, Rotterdam. S. Whitworth Gallery, Manchester.
Doorway of Genoa Cathedral, with Lion. $11^{7/8}$" x $6^{7/16}$" W 1851. V & A
Dordrecht. S 1845. Hereford Gallery.
Dordrecht. W *
Dordt. W 1869
Dordt, from the Maas. W *
Dorre Ville, Geneva/Genoa?. $17^{1/4}$" x $7^{3/4}$" O.
Dover. W x 2 *
Dover Beach. W x 5 *
Dover Beach and Town. W *
Dover Castle. W *
Dover from Blacklands. $21^{1/4}$" x $14^{7/8}$" W 1846.
Dover Harbour. W *
Dover Pier, low water, sunset. 12" x 10" O.
Dover, the White Cliffs. $5^{7/8}$" x $9^{5/8}$" W 31 Aug 1841. Fitzwilliam.

Drawbridge, Rotterdam. W *
Drawing Room, Knole, The. W *
Ducal Palace, Venice, The. W *
Dutch Canal, A. O 1846
Dutch Ferry Boat, Amsterdam, A. O (poss W) 1846
Eastbourne (x 2). W 1868
Eastbourne. S x 2 *
Eelpots. W *
Effect after Rain, Venice. $9^{1/2}$" diameter S 1852
Emma's Hope - Sailing boats & river at dawn. $13^{1/4}$" x $9^{1/2}$" W.
Emma's Hope. W.
English Burial Ground, Lisbon. W *
English Landscape. 49.5cms x 78.7cms O. Leicester City Museum.
Entrance of the Douro. $9^{7/8}$" x $15^{3/4}$" W 28 Aug 1837. V & A
Entrance to the Brown Gallery, Knole. W *
Entrance to the Grand Canal, Venice, Evening, The. (x 2) W 1834.
Entrance to the Grand Canal, Venice. $14^{3/4}$" x $24^{1/2}$" O.
Equestrian Statue. W
Eros Horloge, Rouen, The. W *
Estrella Church, Lisboa. W Jun 1837.
Evening. O 1834
Evening, after Rain. O 1851
Evening. W
Evening. W Sep 1863.
Evening on the Adriatic. $19^{1/4}$" circle O.
Evening, Trafalgar Square. W 1850
Farnese Gardens, Genoa. W *
Fasnakyle, Scotland. W 12 Sep 1853.
Fiesta, Venice, A. W 1860
Figures on a beach resting by a boat. W 11 Sep
Figures Paddling. W 10 Sep 1861. (Eastbourne?)
Fisherfolk Unloading the Catch. $12^{1/4}$" x 18" O.
Fisherman's Song, The. W 1869
Fishing boats on the beach. (C) 10" x 8" W 1860s?
Fishing Boats, Venice, 1857. W *
Fishing for Minnows. W 1837
Fish Market, Venice, The. W 1869
Fish Market, Venice, The. W x 2 *
Fitz Alan Sepulchral Chapel (Arundel Castle). 12" x 20" sketch with wash 1834. British Museum.
Flowers. O V & A 1912-1900
Flowers. W Stoke City Art Gallery
Flowers. S 1825
Flowers. S 1826
Flowers. O 1828
Flowers. W 1828 (x 2)
Flowers. W 1829 (x 2)
Flowers. W 1830. Stoke City Art Gallery
Flowers. O 1838
Flowers. O 1841
Flowers. O 1848 (x 2)
Flowers. W (x 21) Fitzwilliam Museum, including 1 dated 1820 of tulips, etc; 1 dated 1843 of various
        flowers in a Japanese vase and one dated 1839.
Flowers, birds nest and jug. 11" x $19^{3/4}$" W
Flowers, Sketches from Nature. $10^{1/4}$" x $18^{3/4}$" OS 1828. Stoke City
Flower studies. 6" x 7" W (pair).
Flowers, white lilies, and fruit. W.
Flowers, yellow lilies, and fruit. W.
Flowers, in a blue and white dish. W *
Flowers, in a tumbler. W *
Flowers, in a vase. 8" x 15" W. British Museum.
Flowers, in a vase. 8" x 15" W July 1864. British Museum.
Flowers, in a vase. $10^{1/2}$" x $6^{3/4}$" W. Eton College.
Flowers, Wild. W 1828.
Folkestone Pier. W *
Fountain at Innsbruck. W 1858
Fountain Di S.Giorgio, Genoa. O 1858
Fountain of St.George, Genoa. W 1 Oct 1851.
Fountain of St.George, Genoa. $9^{1/4}$" x $5^{1/4}$" W 6 Oct 1851.
Foz, Oporto, The. W *
France from an English Farmyard at Dover. $10^{1/4}$" x $6^{3/4}$" S/W 23 Sep 1846.
Franciscan Convent, Cintra, The. O 1844
Frankfurt. W 1835
Frankfurt. W 1836
Front View of Greenwich Hospital. O 1833
Fruit. W 1828 (x 3).
Fruit. O 1829 (x 2).
Fruit and Flowers. O 1828

Fruit and Flowers. O 1829
Fruit and Flowers. O 1830
Fruit Market near the Rialto. W *
Fruit Market, Venice, A. W 1865
Gateway. O 1832
Gateway to a house. W
Geneva. W 1851 *
Geneva. W 1852
Geneva. W x 3 *
Geneva. Looking South East. W 1869
Genoa (2 views) W 1856
Genoa. W x 2 *
Genoa, October 4th 1851. W *
Genoa Cathedral. W 1851
Genoa from the Bay. O 1852
Genoa from the East Rampart. O Sep 1851
Genoa from the East Rampart. W 1866
Genoa from the Sea. W *
Genoa from the Sea. 24" x 10" W. Eton College.
Genoa from the shore to the North. $12^{1/8}$" x $6^{1/2}$" W.
Genoa, morning. W *
Genoa, near the Palazzo of Andrea Di Doria. W 1869
Genoa, Strada Balbi. $3^{3/4}$" x 5" W. Huntington Library.
Genoa Street Scene. W 1857.
Genoese Boat, A. W *
Gesuati Chiesa, Overra S.Maria Del Rosaris (Venice). W 1858
Gipsy. S 1834
Giudecca, The - a South Wind after Rain. W 1865
Giudecca, Venice. W. Leeds Art Gallery.
Giudecca, Venice. W. Manchester Art Gallery.
Gleam of Sunlight, A. W 1866
Glen, The. W *
Glen Affaric. W *
Glen, Betws-y-Coed, The. W 1863
Glen in North Wales. O 1856
Gondola Race, A. O 1845
Gondolas and Buildings, Venice. W *
Gondolas and People.
Graca Convent, Lisbon, The. W *
Grand Canal, Venice. $6^{5/8}$" x $11^{3/4}$" O prob 1835. Stoke City Gallery
Grand Canal, Venice. W 1843
Grand Canal, Venice. 29" x 18" W. Tate Gallery
Grand Canal, Venice. O 1848
Grand Canal, Venice. O. Leeds Art Gallery.
Grand Canal, Venice. $11^{1/2}$" diameter. O 1853
Grand Canal, Venice. O 1856
Grand Canal, Venice. O. J.R.Rose.
Grand Canal, Venice. 17" x $11^{1/2}$" W.
Grand Canal, Venice. W. Manchester Art Gallery
Grand Canal, Venice. W. Glasgow Art Gallery
Grand Canal, Venice, with two Ladies. W
Grand Canal and Santa Maria Della Salute. $20^{1/4}$" x 14" W 7 Oct 1857 4 p.m. Eton College.
Grapes. W 1828.
Greek Church, Venice, The. O 1848
Greenhill. W 1860 *
Greenwich Hospital. 12" x 8" O. Tate Gallery
Greenwich Hospital. 12" x 9" O
Greenwich Hospital. 12" x 18" W 1831. Museum of London
Greenwich Hospital. $11^{3/4}$" x $8^{3/4}$" W. Same view as above
Greenwich Hospital. $53^{1/4}$" x 35" W 1833
Greenwich Hospital as it was in 1837. O 1867
Greenwich Hospital from the North. $15^{3/4}$" x 11" W 1830/31. National Maritime Museum
Greenwich Hospital from the River. 12" x 18" O 1825. National Maritime Museum/Royal Naval College
Greenwich Hospital, King William's Quadrangle. 9" x 12" W 1837
Greenwich Hospital, King William's Quadrangle. 14" x $10^{1/2}$". National Maritime Museum.
Greenwich Hospital, Painted Hall. $11^{1/2}$" x $8^{7/16}$" S 1839. Huntington Library
Greenwich Hospital, Painted Hall. 10" diameter. National Maritime Museum
Greenwich Hospital, Queen Mary's Colonnoade. 10" x $14^{1/4}$* W
Greenwich Hospital, Queen Marys Quadrangle. 14" x $10^{1/2}$" O. National Maritime Museum. Nb one of the Greenwich
          paintings was presented to the Museum by a Mrs Hillier. It was painted in 1850
Greenwich Hospital, The Arcade with Pensioners Talking. $7^{3/4}$" x $5^{3/8}$" W 8 Jan 1836.
Greenwich Hospital with balloon flying over. $11^{1/2}$" x 9" W.
Greenwich Pensioner. W 1831
Greenwich Pensioner. O 1831
Greenwich Pensioners. O (poss W) 1843
Greenwich. $6^{1/2}$" x $4^{3/16}$" S. Huntington Library.
Group of Flowers, A. W 1824

Hampton Court, May Day. 25" x 21" O.
Harbour, Genoa, The. W *
Harbour, Genoa, The; moonlight. W *
Hastings Beach. S 1847
Heath Scene. 8$^{3}/_{4}$" x 13$^{1}/_{4}$" W. V & A
Hedge Side, The. W 1835
Heiligenblut, Tyrol. W *
Herne Bay. O. Manchester Art Gallery.
Herne Bay. 10$^{1}/_{2}$" x 14$^{1}/_{4}$" S 1834. Huntington Library.
Herne Bay. W 1847
Herne Bay with Shipping. 10$^{3}/_{4}$" x 15$^{1}/_{2}$" S. Huntington Library.
Highborn Maiden, A. W 1866
Hillfield House. 28" x 16$^{3}/_{4}$" O.
Hollyhock. 14$^{3}/_{4}$" x 9$^{3}/_{4}$" W 1853.
Hollyhocks. O 1840
Hollyhocks, from Nature (x 2). W 1828
Hospital for Mendicants, Venice, The. 24" x 35" O 1861
Hospital of the Pieta, Venice. 15$^{1}/_{8}$" x 9$^{7}/_{8}$" W 1844. V & A
House at Greenwich. 17$^{1}/_{4}$" x 12" W 1839. Huntington Library.
House Where Titian was Born, The. O 1860
Hyde Park Corner & Constitution Arch. 35$^{1}/_{2}$" x 21$^{1}/_{4}$" O 1833. Museum of London.
Igreja da Conceicao Velha, A. O. Lisbon City Museum.
Ilfracombe. W 1849. * Stoke City Art Gallery
Ilfracombe. 20" x 14" W 15 Aug 1849. Leeds Gallery
Ilfracombe. W x 2 *
In a French Town. W. Nottingham Castle Museum.
Innsbruck 11$^{3}/_{4}$" x 11$^{3}/_{4}$" W.
Innsbruck. W 24 Aug 1857.
Innsbruck 14" x 11" (x 2) W 1858
In the Church of St.Rogue, Lisbon. O 1848
Interior of a Cathedral, 1837. W *
Interior of a Church, Heiligenblut. W *
Interior of a Church, Innsbruck. W *
Interior of a Cottage, North Wales. W *
Interior of a House. W 183?. Leeds Art Gallery.
Interior of a Panelled Hall and Staircase. W.
Interior of a Studio. W *
Interior of Milan Cathedral. W x 2 *
Interior of Portugese Church. W. Manchester Art Gallery.
Interior of Rouen Cathedral. W *
Interior of SS.Giovanni e Paolo. W x 4 *
Interior of St.Mark's, Venice. S. Leeds Art Gallery.
Interior of St.Mark's, Venice. W x 5 *
Interior of St.Martin, Rouen. W *
Interior of St.Stephen's, Vienna. W *
Interior of the Church of St.Vincent, Rouen. W *
Interior of the Convent, Pentra. W *
Inver Canoch, Inverness-Shire. O 1859
In Venice. 14" x 10" W.
In Venice, Tasso's Echoes are no More. W 1859
Italian Peasant-woman, An. W *
Italian Village. O. Graves Gallery, Sheffield.
Italy. O 1843
Italy, Piazza in an Italian Town. OS.
Keele. W 1863 *
Kensington Gardens. W 1843. V & A?
Kent, Weald of. 10" x 5" S 1834. Huntington Library.
Kingfisher's Haunt, Lord Leigh's Park, Worcestershire, The. W 1867
Kingsdown. W *
Knight's Tomb, The. 10$^{3}/_{4}$" x 8$^{7}/_{8}$" W 1831.
Knole Gallery. W *
Knole House. S 1846
Knole Interior. W. *
Knole, The Cartoon Gallery. 14"$^{1}/_{4}$ x 19$^{1}/_{4}$" unfinished pencil and W Sep 1841. Stoke City Art Gallery.
Knole, Part of East Front. 14$^{3}/_{4}$" x 10$^{1}/_{2}$" W.
Ladies Seated in a Courtyard. 16$^{1}/_{2}$" x 10$^{3}/_{4}$" W 1853.
Lady Betty Germain's Apartment at Knole, The. O. Sissinghurst Castle Kent
Lady Betty Germain's Apartment at Knole, The. W 1845. *
Lago da se Velha, Coimbra, Portugal. 21" x 15" O 1838.
Lago di Garda. W *
Lake Scene, A. W *
Lake Garda: Night Scene. 27.3 cm x 44.5 cm O 1850. Montreal Museum of Fine Art.
Lake Geneva - Head of. O 1844. Graves Gallery, Sheffield.
Lake of Geneva (with Childe Harold quotation). W 1844
Lake of Lucerne, The. O 1845
Landscape. O 1833
Landscape. W 1837

Landscape with Buildings and Trees. $5^{1/2}$" x $10^{1/8}$" W. V & A
Langford Family in their Drawing Room, The. $23^{1/2}$" x $32^{1/2}$" O 1841.
Leaning Tower of the Church of St.George the Greek, Venice, The. W 1845
Leaves from the "Dodger". W 1866
Leicester Gallery, Knole House, Kent, The. O 1843
Leiria. W. Used in "Tourist in Portugal".
Leiria. 7" x $10^{1/4}$" W 1837. V & A
Lierico. W *
Light and Shade. W 1867
Lighthouse, The.
Lilies, Paeony, Delphinium, etc. $15^{1/2}$" x $9^{1/2}$" W 22 Jul 1823. Stoke City Art Gallery
Lion of St.Mark's, The. O 1863
Lion of St.Mark's, The. $18^{1/4}$" x $13^{1/2}$" W 1866.
Lisboa. W 1839
Lisbon, At. W 1839
Lisbon. W *
Lisbon from Port Brandes. O. Manchester Art Gallery.
Lisbon from Port Brandes. S 1839
Lisbon from Port Brandes. W. Lisbon City Museum.
Lisbon from Porto Branko. W *
Liscard Mill, Liverpool. S 1828
Liscard Mill, Liverpool. O 1831
Little Fulling Mill, North Wales, The. W 1866
Llangollyn. O. Stoke City Art Gallery
Llyn Idwal. W 1866
Llyn-y-Dinas. 14" x $9^{3/4}$" W. Stoke City Art Gallery.
Loch Affaire. W *
Loch Benevian. W 1858. *
Loch Benevian. W *
London Bridge. 45.7 cm x 26 cm W. Cleveland Museum of Art.
London from Blackheath. $8^{1/2}$" x $11^{1/4}$" W 1832. Harris Gallery, Preston.
London from Blackheath. O 1834
London from Blackheath. 11.4 cm x 25.6 cm W 1831. National Gallery of Canada, Ottawa.
London from the Thames, showing Somerset House. 29" x 25" O c.1840.
London Lights after Rain, 5th November. W 1846
Long Pool Lynmouth. $13^{1/2}$" x $20^{3/4}$" W July 1849. Huntington Library.
Lucerne. W. Newport Museum & Art Gallery.
Lutheran Church, Rotterdam, The. W 1867
Luzern. W 1841
Lyn Idwall, North Wales. W *
Lynmouth. 30" x 20" W 22 August 1849. British Museum.
Lynmouth. $13^{5/8}$" x $20^{1/2}$" S/W 23 August 1849.
Lynmouth. W x 2 *
Lynmouth Harbour. W *
Lynmouth, North Devon. W x 2 *
Lynmouth. O 1856
Mafra from the Penha Convent. $11^{3/4}$" x 17" W 1846. Huntington Library.
Mafra, Church Interior. $11^{3/4}$" x 17" W. Huntington Library.
Maidstone churchyard. W 22.7.1845.
Maidstone, Gateway. $6^{3/4}$" x $9^{3/4}$" W 1844.
Majesties King William IV & Queen Adelaide, Their, visiting Greenwich Hospital, August 1835. W 1845
Margate (x 2) W 1863
Margate. S *
Margate. W 23 Aug 1859
Margate. W 23 Sep 1861
Margate Beach. W *
Margate Sands. W x 2, one dated 15 Sep*
Margate Sands. 5" x 16" W 5 Sep 1856. (One of the above?)
Margate - The Cannon taken at Sebastopol. W 1859.
Marialva Palace, Cintra. 30.2 cm x 43.7 cm W 1846. * National Gallery of Canada, Ottawa.
Marialva Palace. $5^{3/4}$" x $11^{5/8}$" W 1837. * V & A
Marigold, A. $6^{1/2}$" x $9^{1/2}$" W 1829. Huntington Library.
Marino Faliero, Doge of Venice. O 1854
Marino Faliero's Palace, Venice. W 1857
Market Day, Genoa. W 1856
Market Over. W 1870
Market Scene. O Stoke City Art Gallery.
Mausoleum of Don Emanuel, Batalha. S. Used in "Tourist in Portugal".
Mausoleum of Don Emanuel, never completed, Batalha. W 9 Aug 1837*
Mid-Day. W 1869
Mid-day, Venice. W *
Middle Aisle of the Cathedral of Milan during the Festival of St.Carlo, Borromeo, The. O 1845
Milan. W 1869
Milan Cathedral. S 1840
Milan, Interior of the Cathedral. $7^{1/4}$" x $8^{1/4}$"
Mill on the Rhone, Geneva. $13^{1/2}$" x $9^{1/2}$" W 1841. Fine Art Society.
Milton Chucrh, Gravesend. W 1841

Moel Siabod. W *
Mole Light at Genoa, The. W 1858. *
Monastery of Batalha. W *
Monk, A. W *
Mont Blanc from Ferney. W 1837
Mont Blanc from the Lake of Geneva. W 1837
Monument of Bartolommeo Colleoni. W 1845
Monument of Don John, Batalha. W. Used in "Tourist in Portugal".
Monument of Virgilio Eurisace. $10^{1/2}$" x $19^{1/4}$" W 1850
Moonlight. W 1856
Moorish Castle, Mafra, from the Penha. 17" x $11^{3/4}$" W 21 July 1837. V & A
Moorish Palace, Cintra. $11^{3/4}$" x 17" W 9 July 1837. * V & A
Morning Concert, Palace of Phillipe le Bel. 18" x $11^{1/2}$" O 1849
Morning Concert, A. S 1850
Mountain Stream, North Wales, A. W *
Mountainous Landscape with Rocky Stream (Wales)$14^{3/8}$"x $20^{3/4}$" W 18/9/1855 Cecil Higgins Gallery, Bedford
Mountains near Genoa. W. *
Mountains of the Tyrol, Murano. W
Mouth of a River. $5^{1/8}$" x $9^{1/2}$" W 1830
Mouth of the Bisagno, Genoa. O 1853
Mouth of the Douro. W x 2 *
Mouth of the Lyn. W 1864
Mrs Belem's Hotel Cintra. W. Walker Gallery Liverpool.
Munich. W Aug 1857.
My Ladies Maids at Morning - A Repast at Noon. W 1865
My Lady's Amanuensis. W 1845
Nant Mill, Caernarvonshire. 30" x 20" W 26 Sep 1855. British Museum.
Nant Mill, North Wales. W 1869 *
Naples. $9^{1/4}$" x $15^{7/8}$" W. Stoke City Art Gallery.
Near Marlow. $13^{1/4}$" x $9^{1/2}$" O 1846. Fine Art Society.
Near Pantaleone, Venice. W *
Near S.Pier d'Arena, Genoa. W *
Near the Rialto, Venice. O 1848
Near the Rialto, Venice. W *
Nellie Nick (Charlotte Morrant). O 1853.
Nelson Square, Greenwich. S 1834
New Moon, The - Greenwich Hospital from the River. $10^{3/4}$" dia O June 1852.
Niederdorf. W *
Nimeguen on the Rhine. O 1837
North Entrance of the Palace of Andrea Donia, Genoa. W 1856
North Wales. W 1865
North Wales, mountain scene with sheep. 24" x 12" W. Albany Gallery.
North Wales, The Salmon Trap. $14^{1/4}$" x $19^{1/2}$" W 7 Sep 1855. Stoke City Art Gallery.
Notre Dame, Rouen. W *
Novice, The. O 1844
Nun giving a coin to a beggar in a church doorway.
Nymegen. O V & A 80
Nymegen. $6^{1/4}$" x $10^{1/8}$" W. V & A FA47.
Oakhurst; the seat of C F Huth, Esq. W *
Off Greenwich, a Recollection. W 1863
Off the Lido, St.Agnes' Eve. O 1857
Old Archway, Batalha. W *
Old Buildings and Trees. W *
Old Buildings, Rouen. W *
Old Cathedral, Coimbra, The. S. Used in "Tourist in Portugal".
Old Church, Betws-y-Coed. W *
Old Church, Rouen. W *
Old Cottage and Figures, North Wales. W *
Old House with Figures, An.
Old Mill at Blackheath, An. W 1835
Old Mole, Genoa, The. W *
On Lake Geneva. W *
On the Coast at Deal. W *
On the Coast, Oporto. W *
On the Grand Canal. O 1855
On the Grand Canal, Venice. W x 2 *
On the Ravensbourne. O 1844
On the River Colne, "The Tile House", the seat of Mortimer Drummond Esq, in the Distance. O 1843
On the River Cray. W *
On the River Maas. O 1847
On the River Ravensbourne, Kent. W 1841
On the River Tagus. W 1848
On the River Tay. W 1835
On the River Thames below Woolwich. S 1843
On the Cray, Kent. W 1869
On the Thames below Greenwich. S 1850
On the Thames. W *

On the Thames - Mill Tail. W 1865
Oporto. 7" x 10$^{1/8}$" W 1837. V & A
Oporto. S. Used in "Tourist in Portugal".
Oporto. W x 2 *
Oporto from St.Johns. S. Used in "Tourist in Portugal".
Opposite the Leone Bianca, Venice. W *
Ospedale Civile, Venice. 16$^{1/8}$" x 27$^{3/16}$" W 1858. V & A
Os Pisoes, Cintra (The Fulling Mill). 6$^{3/4}$" x 10" W 1837. V & A
Paddle Steamer by Pier at Margate. W
Palace of La Reine, Blanche. O 1849
Palace le Rene, Blanche, Paris - A summer residence of Blanche la Belle. W
Palace of Phillipe le Bel. W 1831
Palace of Phillipe le Bel. O. National Museum of Wales, Cardiff.
Palais des Papes, Avignon. 11$^{3/4}$" x 7$^{3/4}$" W.
Palais le Reine, Paris. W *
Palazzo dei Camerlinghi, Venice. 16$^{3/4}$" x 11$^{3/8}$" W.
Pantheon from the Piazza Della Rotonda, Rome. 14$^{1/4}$" x 10$^{5/8}$" W
Paris, church interior. W
Paris, le Tour de Phillipe de Bel. 1845.
Paris, North door of Notre Dame. 9$^{7/8}$" x 6$^{3/4}$" O 1845. Stoke City Art Gallery
Paris, Notre Dame. W. Newport Museum & Art Gallery
Paris, river scene. C. 10" x 7" W 1838. Fitzwilliam Museum, Cambridge
Paris, Rue St.George. 6$^{1/2}$" x 9$^{1/2}$" S & W. 23 August 1845. Stoke City Art Gallery
Paris, Rue St.Jacques. 9$^{1/4}$" x 7" W 1831.
Paris Street and Church Portal. (S side of Notre Dame). 1831 W.
Paris, Street Scene. 6" x 4" W
Paris, Street Scene. W 1831.
Parrot Tulip, A. 7$^{7/8}$" x 10$^{1/2}$" W 1826.
Part of the Foscari Palace. W 1842
Part of Genoa. O 1853
Part of the Mausoleum of Don Amanuel & Interior of Pentra Convent, Cintra. W 1863
Part of Old Treasury, Lisbon. 13$^{3/4}$" x 10$^{1/8}$" W 2 June 1837 (poss 2 views). V & A
Part of St.Edwards Chapel, with the tombs of Edward III and his Queen, Phillippa. W 1835
Part of the Old Fish Market, Venice. O 1840
Pass D'Ampezzo, Tyrol. W 1860
Peasant Woman at Geneva. W 1835.
Pentra Convent, Cintra, The. W 1837.
Pentra Convent, Cintra, The. W 1839. * Ferens Art Gallery, Hull.
Piazza of St.Marks looking towards the Statue. 10$^{1/2}$" diameter. S 1848 Leeds City Gallery.
Piazza Signori, Verona. W 1844/1835? * Laing Gallery Newcastle.
Piazzetta of St.Marks. 23" x 16" O 1859
Piazzetta San Michele, Verona. W *
Piazzetta, Venice, A. W *
Piazzetta, Venice, The. W x 2 *
Piazetta, Venice, The. O 1862. Art Gallery of WA, Perth.
Picture Gallery, Knole, The. W *
Pine Trees in Mountainous Scenery. W
Ponte del Cavallo, Venice. W *
Ponte del Paradiso, Venice. 5" x 8$^{1/4}$" W. Huntington Library.
Ponte SS.Apostili. W 1859
Pool of Water, with an Angler, A. W *
Poppies. 10$^{1/2}$" x 8$^{1/4}$" W.
Poppies and Lillies. 22" x 16" O 1847.
Porch of a Church, The. W *
Porch of S.Maclou, Rouen. W *
Porch of St.Vincent, Rouen, with figures, The. W *
Port of Genoa. O. Walker Gallery Liverpool.
Porto de Moz. S. Used in "Tourist in Portugal".
Porto de Moz. 16$^{3/4}$" x 11$^{1/2}$" W 8 August 1837. * V & A
Portrait of a Woman in Blue. 5" x 10" W 29 October 1861. British Museum.
Portrait of Women at Devotions. 14" x 11$^{1/4}$"
Portugal? Location unknown. W 1837. Stoke City Art Gallery. P 1990.
Portugal 1859.
Portugal sketches 1837. Fitzwillian Museum, Cambridge.
Portugal sketches 1837. Walker Art Gallery, Liverpool.
Post Office, Venice, The. W 1859
Posy of Roses and Other Flowers. 10$^{7/8}$" x 8$^{5/8}$" W.
Procession of the Host, Venice. W *
Provencal Street Scene. 13$^{1/4}$" x 9$^{3/8}$" W. Eton College.
Quay, The. 5" x 7" W. V & A
Quay in Front of the Doges' Palace. 19$^{1/2}$" x 11$^{1/2}$" S 1854
Ramsgate, near the Harbour. 8$^{1/4}$" x 12$^{1/2}$" W. V & A
Recollection of the Festival of the Church of St.Maria della Salute, Venice. 11" x 7" O.
Recollection of Venice. 16$^{1/2}$" x 11$^{1/2}$" W. Tate Gallery.
Recollection of Venice. O. Birmingham Art Gallery.
Recollection of Venice, Evening. O 1847
Recollections of a Venetian Canal. O 1853

Regent's Park. O. Spink and Son 1984.
Remains of a Moorish Mosque at Cintra. W *
Remains of the Ampitheatre, Verona. W 1842
Remains of the Church of St.Joseph, Lisbon. O 1843
Remains of the Palace La Reine Blanche. O 1831
Retiring of the Council of Ten, The. O 1846
Return, The. S 1842
Returning from Church, Venice. W *
Returning from Market, Dordrecht. O 1846
Returning from the Shrine. $22^{1/2}$" x 16" S 1862
Rialto, The. $4^{1/2}$" x $6^{1/8}$" S & W.
Rialto, The. 21" x 30" W. Fine Art Society.
Rialto, The. 38" x 58" O 1859. Fine Art Society
Rialto, The. O 1859.
Rialto, The. $7^{1/4}$" x $11^{1/4}$" W. 1857. *
Rialto, The. W 1862
Rialto, The. O. Graves Gallery, Sheffield.
Rialto, The. W. Graves Gallery, Sheffield.
Rialto, The. W. Manchester Art Gallery.
Rialto, The, Venice. 9" x $15^{3/8}$" W 1865. V & A
Rialto, The, Venice. 10" diameter. O 1854
Riva degli Schiavoni, Venice. $9^{1/2}$" diameter W 1865.
Riva degli Schiavoni, Venice. 19.6 cm x 22.6 cm W.
Riva degli Schiavoni, Venice. $6^{1/2}$" x $9^{3/4}$" W.
Rivals, The. W 1865
River Bisagno, Genoa, The. W 1867
River landscape with fishing boats, probably on the Rhine or the Danube. $13^{3/4}$" x 12" O.
River Medway (probably) - Fishing Boats off shore. $8^{1/4}$" x $7^{1/4}$" W 1830. Stoke City Art Gallery.
River Scene. O. Stoke City Art Gallery
River Scene, Delft, A. W *
River Scene in the Tyrol, A. W *
River Scene, North Wales, A. W *
River Scene - Rochester, Kent. $8^{1/2}$" x $15^{1/2}$" W. Harris Gallery, Preston.
River Scene with Boats and Buildings, A. $6^{1/2}$" x $8^{5/8}$" W. V & A
River Scene with a Bridge. W *
River Scene with Windmill. 6" x $9^{5/8}$" W. V & A
Road Scene, North Wales, A. W *
Road Scene, Wales, A. W *
Rocks near Oporto. W *
Rocks on the Coast, Lynmouth. W *
Rocky Landscape, A. W *
Rocky Stream, A. W *
Rose, A. 9" x $6^{1/2}$" W 1829. Huntington Library.
Roses, Convolvulus & Delphinium. $16^{13/16}$" x $11^{11/32}$" W 1839. V & A
Rose and Delphinium. 10" x $14^{3/4}$" W. Huntington Library.
Roses in a Glass. W *
Roses, Poppy, Pelargonia, Delphinium & Calceolarias. 17" x $14^{11/16}$" W1859. V & A
Rotterdam. 24" x 12" W Sep/Oct 1845. British Museum.
Rotterdam. W x 4 *
Rotterdam, October 1843. W *
Rotterdam. $39^{1/2}$" x $59^{1/2}$" O 1849
Rotterdam. 10" x 18" W 30 September 1845. Tate Gallery.
Rotterdam - An October Morning (x 2). S 1849
Rotterdam Canal Scene. 14 " x 11" O 1853. Harris Gallery, Preston.
Rotterdam Canal Scene. W x 2 *
Rotterdam views. W (pair) *
Rouen. 10" x $6^{7/8}$" S 1850.
Rouen. S 1851 plus possibly another in 1856
Rouen, St.Ouen. 10" x 20" S. Tate Gallery.
Rouen, Church of St.Vincent. $16^{1/2}$" x $11^{1/2}$" W. 1 o'clock 22 Aug 1850. Leeds City Art Gallery
Rouen, Church of St.Vincent. 17" x $11^{3/4}$" S & W 25 Aug 1850..
Rouen from the River. S 1855
Rouen, the Clock Tower. $19^{1/8}$" x $13^{1/4}$" W 14 August 1850. V & A
Rouen, Notre Dame. $6^{7/8}$" x 10" W (pair).
Rouen, study of arch. 10" x 20" S 21 August. Tate Gallery.
Rouen Street Scene. W *
Rouen, Tour d'Horloge. 10" x 20" S. Tate Gallery.
Rouen, Tour d'Horloge.$11^{3/4}$" x $6^{3/8}$" S 13 August.
Rough Coast Scene. $14^{1/4}$" x $9^{3/4}$" W. Huntington Library.
Royal Naval College, Greenwich. W 1848. Royal Naval College.
Rua Mezericordia, Leiria, Portugal. $21^{1/2}$" x 15" O 1838.
Rua Nova dos Inglezes. S. Used in "Tourist in Portugal".
Ruined Church, Lisbon. W *
Ruins of San Francisco, Lisbon. W 1837*
Ruins of the Monastery of Alcobaco. W 1839
Ryde Harbour, IOW. $13^{1/2}$" x $6^{1/2}$" W.
Sailors Home, The. O 1843

St.Edward's Chapel, Westminster Abbey. O 1835
St.George Majeur.
St.George's, Venice. $11^{1/2}$" x $22^{1/2}$" W. Harris Gallery, Preston.
St.Georgio Canal, Venice. W 1848
St.Giorgio, Maggiori. O 1841
St.Honrius Cave, Cintra. S 1846. Graves Gallery, Sheffield.
St.Jacques Church, Antwerp (interior). 18" x 10" W 1841.
St.John's, Oporto. W *
St.Joseph's, Lisbon. 17" x $11^{3/4}$" S 1837. Stoke City Art Gallery (pencilled note; "destroyed by the earthquake")
St.Lawrence, Rotterdam. O 1859
St.Lawrence, Rotterdam. W *
St.Lawrence, Rouen. $6^{7/8}$" x 10" S.
St.Lawrence, Rouen. W 14 Aug
St.Maclou, Rouen. $13^{13/16}$" x $9^{7/8}$" W 20 August 1850. Fitzwilliam.
St.Mark's Quay, Venice. W 1857. *
St.Mark's Square, Venice. W 26 Sep 1857
St.Mary's Chapel, Warwick. O 1835
St.Ouen, Rouen. W *
St.Rogue, Lisboa. W
St.Tomaso, Genoa. W x 2 *
St.Severin's, Paris. W. Lady Lever Gallery, Port Sunlight.
St.Stephen's, Vienna. W *
St.Vincent de Rouen. W 1857
St.Vincent, Lisbon. W *
Sailing Boat, Venice. W Sep 1857.
Sailing Boat. W 11 Sep 1861
Sailing Boats. W 26 Oct.
Salmon Leap. O 1858
Salmon Trap, Glyn LLeddr. O 1853. Graves Gallery, Sheffield.
Salmon Trap. W *
Salute, Venice. W. Manchester Art Gallery
San Francisco (Portugal). $11^{5/8}$" x $16^{3/4}$" W 1 July 1837. V & A
San Giorgio, Venice. $18^{1/2}$" x $14^{1/4}$" W. Derby Art Gallery
San Marco Venice, W 1 October 1845. Harrow School
San Marco Venice. 1859.
San P. d'Arena and the Lighthouse, Genoa. W *
San Pier d'Arena, Genoa. W *
Santa Cruz, Coimbra. W 1841 *
Santa Maria Della Salute. O 1845
Santa Maria Della Salute. W x 2 *
Santa Maria Della Salute and Gondola. $11^{1/2}$" x $2^{1/2}$" W 1865. Harris Gallery Preston
Santa Maria, San Miguel, Cintra. 10" x $6^{3/4}$" S 1837. Stoke City Art Gallery
Scaligeri Monument, Venice, The. W 1863. Manchester Art Gallery
Scaligeri Monument, Verona, The. W. Manchester Art Gallery
Scene in Switzerland, A. W *
Scene in the Val d'Ampezzo. W *
Scene in Venice. W 1840. Manchester Art Gallery.
Scene near the Hague, Sunset. S 1847
Scene on the Darent. S 1834
Seascape with Rainbow, Deal to Kingsdown. W 16 Sep 1849
Seashore with Figures (Ilfracombe?). W Oct 1861. Manchester Art Gallery.
Sea View. O 1834
Sedan Chair, The. W 1865
Seminary from the Freixo, The. W. Used in "Tourist in Portugal"
Serra Convent. W. Used in "Tourist in Portugal"
Shakespeare's Cliff, Dover. W 1847 *
Shakespeare's Cliff, from Folkestone. W *
Shipping, Bathing Machines, etc. W 1834
Shipping in a cove at dusk. $12^{1/2}$" x $11^{3/4}$" SW.
Ships and Clouds. 8" x $12^{3/4}$" W 13 Sep 1849. Huntington Library.
Shrine of St.Agnes, The. W 1862
Side Canal, Venice, A. $10^{7/8}$" x $7^{3/8}$" W 1835. Fitzwilliam, Cambridge.
Sketch for a picture. S 1840
Sketch of San Marco, Venice. W. Manchester Art Gallery.
Sketch of Wild Flowers - Composition. S 1827
Snowdon. W 18 September 1855. Cecil Higgins Gallery, Bedford.
Snowdon. W x 3 *
Snowdon from Moel Siabod. W *
Snowdon, Sunset. W *
South Door, Notre Dame, Rouen. W *
S.Pier Da Arena, Geneva. S 1853
S.Pier Da Aerna, Genoa. O 1860
Southend Bridge. O 1832
South Wind, St.John's, Oporto, A. W. *
Spangled Bedroom, Knole House, Kent, The. O 1843
Spanish Building. W *
Spanish Lady. 13" x $8^{1/4}$" W 21 Jul 1858. Stoke City Art Gallery

Spanish Lady at her Devotion, A. W *
Spanish Vineyard, A. W *
Square in Venice, A. W *
SS.Giovani & Paolo Venice - A Small Chapel. W 1863
Stream in North Wales, A. W *
Street of Misericordia, Leiria. S. Used in "Tourist in Portugal"
Street Scene at Night. W 26 Oct 1849.
Street Scene, Genoa. O 1867
Street Scene, Genoa, A. W 1857*
Street Scene, Rotterdam, A. W x 2 *
Street Scene, Rouen, A. W *
Street Scene with a Fruit Stall, Oporto, A. W *
Street Scene with Archway, October 2nd. W
Striped tulip. 7" x 9" W
Street Scene in Rouen, A. W.
Studies at the Seaside. W 1861
Study, A. W 1832
Study from Nature. W 1829
Study from Nature. O 1832
Study from Nature. W 1834 (x 2)
Study from Nature. O 1835
Study in the Woods at Plumstead. W 1834
Study of a Boat. W *
Study of a Boat, Deal. W 18 Sep 1849.
Study of a Building. W 24 Oct 1857 (Venice)
Study of a Fir Tree. W *
Study of a Rainbow. W *
Study of Arches with figures.
Study of Boats, Oporto. W *
Study of Boats, Venice. W *
Study of Boats with figures. W
Study of Cliffs, Dover Beach. W *
Study of Clouds. W 20 Sep.
Study of Clouds. W Sep 1861
Study of Deal. W *
Study of Flowers. O 1830
Study of Flowers. O 1836
Study of Flowers after Nature. W 1827
Study of Folkestone. W *
Study of Fruit. O 1829
Study of Fruit. O 1830
Study of Light, A - Knole. W 1865
Study of Rocks and Trees. W (erased) *
Study of Rocks, Ilfracombe. W x 3 *
Study of Roses in my Garden at Blackheath 1839. W 1869
Study of Sea. W x 2 *
Study of the Belladonna Lily, after Nature. S 1826
Study of Trees. W x 2
Study of Trees and Figures. W *
Study of the French Coast from Dover, A. 6$^{1/2}$" x 9$^{3/4}$" W Aug 1846.
Summer. W 1847
Summer - Venice. W 1868
Sunset. W 1847
Sunset. O 1854
Sunet on Italian Coast. W 1853. Whitworth Gallery, Manchester.
Sunset on the Medway. W 1830.
Sunset over the Estuary. 9$^{1/2}$" x 5$^{1/4}$" W. Huntington Library.
Sunset, Rouen. W 24 Aug 1850
Sunshine, Venice. W 1865
Tagus, The. S 1840
Temple Museum Leeds. O 1848.
Terrace, Cintra, A. W *
Thames at Greenwich, The. W *
Thames at Greenwich, The. 10$^{1/4}$" x 17" W.
Thames below Woolwich, The. 24" x 20" W 1843. Tate Gallery.
Thames near Marlow, The. W *
Tombs of the Scaligers at Verona. S 1852
Tombs of the Scaligers, Verona. W *
Torcello. W x 2 *
Torre da Marco. 11$^{3/4}$" x 17" W 28 Aug 1837. * V & A
Torre dos Clerigos, Oporto. 16$^{3/8}$" x 11$^{1/2}$" W 26 Aug 1837. V & A
Torres Vedras. 11$^{3/4}$" x 16$^{1/2}$" W 1838. * V & A
Tower of the Clergy. W. Used in "Tourist in Portugal".
Tower of London by night with fireworks. 18" x 1$^{1/2}$" O.
Townfolk in a Street with Classical Buildings (Paris).6$^{1/2}$" X 4$^{1/4}$" S 1831.
Trafalgar Square. W *
Treath Mawr. W *

Trentham Hall from The Lake. W. Stoke City Art Gallery
Trentham Park, Staffs. W/S
Treves. W *
Trout Stream, Kent, A. W 1841
Tulip, Dog Rose and "Love-in-a-Mist". $8^{1/2}$" x $10^{1/2}$" W 1830. Stoke City Art Gallery
The Tyrol. W 1869
Upper Pool from Limehouse. W
Val d'Ampezzo. W x 6 *
Venetian Backwater, A. $16^{1/4}$" x $10^{1/4}$" W.
Venetian Bedroom, Knole, The. W 1865
Venetian Canal, A. $13^{3/8}$" x $19^{3/4}$" W. Ulster Museum, Belfast.
Venetian Capricio. W. Walker Gallery Liverpool
Venetian Island. $8^{1/2}$" x $12^{1/2}$" W.
Venetian Room, Knole, The. W *
Venetian Scene (Rednetore Chrurch Guidecca). $50^{1/4}$" x $30^{1/4}$" W. Fine Art Society.
Venetian Sketch. W. Stoke City Art Gallery.
Venetian Woman, A. W. *
Venetien. W 1856
Venezia. O 1863
Venezia. 11" x 20" W 22 Oct 1857.
Venezia (x 2). W 1864
Venice. J Orrock Collection.
Venice. $23^{1/2}$" x $19^{1/2}$" O 1839. Stoke City Art Gallery.
Venice. $11^{1/2}$" x $7^{3/4}$" O.
Venice. O. Manchester Art Gallery.
Venice from the Giudecca. W 1840. Manchester City Gallery.
Venice. 10" x 6" S 1845.
Venice. S. Leeds Art Gallery.
Venice. S 1850
Venice. O. Leeds Art Gallery.
Venice. O 1851. Stoke City Art Gallery.
Venice. O x 2. Stoke City Art Gallery.
Venice. 4" x $2^{1/4}$" W 1856. Stoke City Art Gallery. This painting was removed from its frame in the late 1980s to
    reveal a poem in the artist's hand. It was valued by Sothebys in 1980 at £100, before the existence of the
    poem was known.
Venice. $18^{1/2}$" x $12^{1/2}$" W.
Venice. W x 3 *
Venice. W 1857. Cardiff.
Venice. W. Worcester Art Gallery.
Venice, with shipping. (c) 24" x 18" W 1857. Fitzwilliam, Cambridge.
Venice. W 1857. Walker Gallery, Liverpool.
Venice. W 1857. Temple Museum, Leeds.
Venice. W 1 Oct 1857. Laing Gallery, Newcastle.
Venice. W 30" x 20" 30 October 1857. British Museum.
Venice. 20" x 10" W. British Museum.
Venice. 14" x $20^{1/4}$" W 30 Sep 1857. Cecil Higgins, Bedford.
Venice. 15" x 23" W. Fine Art Society.
Venice. W 1841.
Venice. W 1863. Manchester City Gallery.
Venice. W.
Venice, a narrow canal. $9^{3/4}$" x $6^{1/2}$" O 1859. Stoke City Art Gallery.
Venice, a SW wind after Rain. $6^{7/8}$" x $10^{3/8}$" W 1864. V & A
Venice, Across the Lagoon with the Campanile & St.Marks. $18^{1/4}$" x $28^{1/4}$" W. Stoke City Art Gallery.
Venice, Canal. 15" x $10^{3/4}$" W. Huntington Library.
Venice, Canal Scene. W x 3 *
Venice, Canal Scene. W.
Venice, the Dogana. $17^{1/2}$" x $36^{1/4}$" W 1864. Huntington Library.
Venice, the Dogana. $17^{1/4}$" x 10" W. Huntington Library.
Venice Eveving. $19^{3/4}$" x 11" W 1836. Fine Art Society.
Venice Evening. W 1848
Venice from the Lagoon. $7^{7/8}$" x $12^{5/8}$" pen and brush.
Venice from St.Giorgio; sketched from a Gondola, October 1857. W *
Venice from St.Giorgio. W 1864
Venice, St.Mark's Interior. 10" x 6" W Oct 1857
Venice, The Fish Market. $6^{1/4}$" x $13^{3/4}$" O prob 1835. Stoke City Art Gallery.
Venice, The Giudecca. 6" x $8^{1/2}$" W 1857. Leeds Gallery.
Venice, The Giudecca. W. Leeds Gallery.
Venice, Gondola Moorings. $6^{1/2}$" x $9^{1/4}$" W 25 Sep. Huntington Library.
Venice, Grand Canal. $28^{1/4}$" x $18^{1/2}$" O.
Venice, seen from across the lagoon. 17.5 cm x 28.3 cm W post 1856. National Gallery of Canada, Ottawa.
Venice, sketches Nov 1850.
Venice, The Lagoon.
Venice, The Lagoon by Moonlight. 10" x 8" O.
Venice Morning. W 1848
Venice, Piazza di San Marco. 11" x 9" O 1850. Royal Holloway College, Egham. Inscribed on the reverse; "To Peter
    Potter, Esq. This picture is a genuine work of Yours Very Truly James Holland, Jan 22, 1855."

Venice, The Salute. 12$^{1}/_{2}$" x 7$^{3}/_{4}$" S. Huntington Library.
Venice, The Statue and The Grand Canal. 9$^{3}/_{4}$" x 13$^{1}/_{2}$" O 1857. Stoke City Art Gallery
Venice, view of Santa Maria Della Salute and Piazzetta de San Marco. W.
Venice, view up the Grand Canal. 35$^{1}/_{2}$" x 26$^{1}/_{2}$" W. Exhibited Royal Jubile Exhibition Manchester 1887 & Burlington House 1901.
Venice, with Baccino with San Giorgio Maggiore. 42" x 24" W.
Venice, with Gondolas and People
Verona. 20" x 10" W 1844. British Museum.
Verona. S 1845. Baroda, India.
Verona. W 1869 *
Verona, The Ampitheatre. 13$^{3}/_{4}$" x 9" W 1835. Stoke City Art Gallery.
Vesper House, The. W 1866
Vesper Time, Venice. W 1862.
Vespers at Maddona Dell Orto. W 1847
Vico Sotto, Il Campanile, Genoa. W 1866
View across the Piazelta towards the Salute. O 1853
View at Dale Park. W *
View from Dover, 1846. W *
View from Greenwich Hospital. O. National Maritime Museum.
View in North Wales, Arenig with Snowdon beyond. 21$^{1}/_{2}$" x 15" W. Washington National Gallery of Art (1993)
View in the Tyrol. W x 2 *
View near Murano. W *
View of a Castle on the Rhone (possibly actually on the Rhine). 14$^{1}/_{2}$" x 12$^{1}/_{2}$" O 1857.
View of Leiria, Portugal, A. 15" x 12$^{1}/_{8}$" O 1838. Cecil Higgins Bedford.
View of London from Blackheath. O 1833
View of Venetian Canal. W. Bristol Art Gallery.
View of the Thames below Greenwich. O 1833
View on a Canal in Venice. 14$^{1}/_{4}$" x 9$^{1}/_{4}$" W 1836.
View on the Douro. W *
View on the Grand Canal. W *
View on the Medway. W 1827
View on the Ravensbourne. W 1833
View on the Ravensbourne. 32$^{1}/_{4}$" x 19$^{3}/_{4}$" O 1843. There was possibly a second oil of the same subject.
Villa do Conde, Portugal. 11$^{3}/_{4}$" x 7" W 2 Sep 1837. V & A
Villa Doria, Genoa, The. W *
Villa Nova. W. Used in "Tourist in Portugal".
Village Church. O 1831
Visit to the Shrine, A. O. Walker Gallery, Liverpool.
Waiting for our Gondola, Murano. S 1859-62.
Walmer. W 1849.
Walmer. S Sep 1849
Walmer Beach. W *
Walmer Castle. O 1850
Walmer Castle. 20$^{1}/_{2}$" x 11" W. * Huntington Library.
Warwick, Stone Arch. 6$^{1}/_{2}$" x 9$^{1}/_{2}$" W. Huntington Library.
Waterfall, The (North Wales?). W 1843.
Watermill, A. W *
Weir at Great Marlow, The. W *
Welsh Mountains. W *
Welsh River Scene, A. W x 4 *
Welsh Road Scene, A. W x 2 *
Welsh Road Scene, with a Cart and Figures, A. W *
Welsh Stream, A. W *
Welsh Valley, A. W *
Welsh Waterfall, 1855, A. W *
Welsh Watermill, A. W x 2 *
Wind from S.W, The. W 1867
Windmill. O. Stoke City Art Gallery.
Windmill with boat. O. Stoke City Art Gallery.
Windy Day, Deal. W 14 Sep 1849.
Women taking their Siesta at the Unfinished Mausoleum of Don Emmanual, Bathala Monastery. W 1837. Whitworth Gallery, Manchester.
Woody Dell. W 1827
Woody Lane, A - Scene. W *
Woody River Scene, with figures, A. W *
Woody Stream, Lynmouth, A. W *
Yachts. c 40" x 30" O. Stoke City Art Gallery.
Zattere, September 21st. W

APPENDIX B: PRESENT OWNERS OF JAMES HOLLAND PICTURES
(Collections accessible by the public)

ASHMOLEAN MUSEUM, OXFORD (7)
Venice, oil; Church of St.Vincent Rouen, sketch; Venice, water-colour; Flowers - Canterbury Bells, water-colour; Addlestone Oak, water-colour; Interior of St.Jacques church Antwerp, water-colour; From nature, sketch.

ART GALLERY OF WESTERN AUSTRALIA, PERTH (1)
The Piazzetta Venice, oil.

BEDFORD, CECIL HIGGINS GALLERY (4)
Mountainous Landscape with Rocky Stream (Snowdon), water-colour 1855;
A View of Leiria, Portugal, oil 1838; Venice, water-colour 1857; Confessor's Chapel Westminster Abbey, water-colour 1834.

BELFAST, ULSTER MUSEUM. (1)
A Venetian Canal, water-colour.

BIRMINGHAM MUSEUM & ART GALLERY (2)
A Recollection of Venice, oil; Canal Scene Venice, oil.

BOSTON MUSEUM OF FINE ART (1)
Church Portal Lisbon, water-colour.

BRISTOL CITY ART GALLERY (1)
View of Venetian Canal, water-colour.

BRITISH MUSEUM (11)
Lynmouth, water-colour 1849; Nant Mill Caernarvonshire, water-colour; Portrait of a Woman in Blue, water-colour 1861; Rotterdam, water-colour; Venice, two water-colours, one dated 1857; Clifton Baths Margate, water-colour; Verona, water-colour 1844; Flowers, two water-colours, one dated 1864; Fitz Alan Sepulchral Chapel (Arundal Castle), sketch 1834.

CARDIFF, NATIONAL MUSEUM OF WALES (3)
Venice, water-colour; Venetian Church, 1844 water-colour; Palace of Philippe le Bel, oil.

CLEVELAND MUSEUM OF ART (1)
London Bridge, water-colour.

DERBY MUSEUM & ART GALLERY (1)
San Giorgio Venice, water-colour.

DUBLIN, MUNICIPAL MUSEUM (2)
Colleoni's Monument, oil. The Ampitheatre at Verona, water-colour (in 1913).

FITZWILLIAM MUSEUM, CAMBRIDGE (29)
Church in Batalha Portugal, water-colour; Cistercian Monastry Alcobaca, water-colour; Dover, water-colour; Paris, river scene, water-colour; St.Maclou Rouen, water-colour; A Side Canal Venice, water-colour; Venice, with shipping water-colour; Convent of Mafra Estremadura Portugal, water-colour; 21 various flower studies, including works dated 1820, 1839 and 1843.

GREENWICH ART GALLERY & MUSEUM (2)
Charlton House, water-colour; Greenwich Hospital from the Thames, water-colour.

HARRIS GALLERY, PRESTON (5)
London from Blackheath, water-colour; Rotterdam Canal Scene, oil; Santa Maria Della Salute and Gondola, water-colour; River Scene Rochester water-colour; St.George's Venice, water-colour.

HEREFORD ART GALLERY & MUSEUM (1)
Dordrecht, water-colour.

HULL, FERENS ART GALLERY (1)
Pentra Convent Cintra, water-colour.

HENRY E.HUNTINGTON LIBRARY & ART GALLERY, LOS ANGELES (32)
Ampitheatre at Verona, water-colour; Antwerp, water-colour; Beach Scene, sketch; Boats and Beach Scene, sketch; Charing Cross, water-colour; Chapel of the Penha, wash; Near Delft, sketch; Dianthus, water-colour; Genoa - Strada Balbi, water-colour; Greenwich Hospital - Great Hall, sketch; Greenwich, sketch; House at Greenwich, water-colour; Herne Bay, sketch; Herne Bay, sketch; Kentish Weald, sketch; Long Pool, Lynmouth, water-colour; Mafra from The Penha Convent, wash; Mafra Church Interior, wash; A Marigold, water-colour; Ponte del Paradiso, sketch; A Rose, water-colour; Rose and Delphinium, water-colour; Rough Coast Scene, water-colour; Ships and Clouds, water-colour; Sunset over The Estuary, water-colour; Venice Canal, water-colour; Venice - The Dogana, water-colour; Venice - The Dogana, water-colour; Venice - Gondola Moorings, water-colour; Venice, the Salute, sketch; Walmer Castle, water-colour; Warwick - Stone Arch, water-colour.

LADY LEVER GALLERY, PORT SUNLIGHT, LIVERPOOL (1)
St.Severin's Paris, water-colour.

LAING GALLERY, NEWCASTLE (3)
Chapel of the Confessors St.Marks, water-colour; La Piazza di Senori Verona, water-colour; Bridge over Canal Venice, water-colour.

LEEDS CITY ART GALLERY (9?)
Grand Canal, oil *; Venice, Piazza of San Marco looking towards the Statue, oil; Venice, the Giudecca, water-colour x 2; Venice, drawing *; Interior of unidentified house, water-colour; Interior of St.Mark's Venice, drawing *; Church of

St.Vincent Rouen, drawing; Deal Seascape, water-colour; (Ilfracombe, water-colour, present in 1960s, but not when contents checked in 1992). This collection includes those held at the Temple Museum. * indicates not seen during 1997 check.

LEGER GALLERIES (1)
Church doorway.

LEICESTER CITY MUSEUM (1)
English Landscape, 1841 oil.

LISBON CITY MUSEUM (2)
A Igreja da Conceicao Velha, oil; Lisboa vista do Porto Brandao, water-colour.

MANCHESTER CITY GALLERY (15)
Lisbon from Porto Brandas, oil *; Venice, oil; Herne Bay, oil; Canal Scene Venice, water-colour *; Grand Canal, water-colour; Scene in Venice, water-colour; Scagliari Monument, water-colour; Sketch of San Marco, water-colour *; Venice from the Giudecca, water-colour *; Salute Venice, water-colour *; Giudecca Venice, water-colour; Rialto, water-colour; Interior of Portugese Church, water-colour; Seashore with Figures, water-colour; Scaligeri Verona, water-colour. * indicates not seen during 3/97 visit.

MONTREAL MUSEUM OF FINE ART (1)
Lake Garda Night Scene, oil.

MUSEUM OF LONDON (3)
Hyde Park Corner & Constitution Arch, oil; Demolition work at the South end of London Bridge, water-colour; Greenwich Hospital, water-colour.

NATIONAL ART GALLERY, WELLINGTON, NEW ZEALAND (1)Beckenham Church Porch, watercolour.

NATIONAL GALLERY OF CANADA, OTTAWA (3)
London from Blackheath, water-colour; Marialva Palace, water-colour; Venice from across the lagoon, water-colour.

NATIONAL MARITIME MUSEUM, GREENWICH (6)
Anniversary Festival of Battle of Trafalgar, water-colour; Greenwich Hospital from the North, water-colour; Greenwich Hospital from the River, oil; Greenwich Hospital Queen Marys Quadrangle, oil; Their Majesties King William IV and Queen Adelaide visiting Greenwich Hospital August 1835, water-colour; View from Greenwich Hospital, water-colour.

NATIONAL TRUST, SISSINGHURST CASTLE (2)
The Brown Gallery Knole, oil; Lady Betty Germain's Apartment Knole, oil.

NEWPORT MUSEUM & ART GALLERY (2)
Lucerne, water-colour; Notre Dame, water-colour.

NOTTINGHAM CASTLE MUSEUM (3)
View in Venice, oil; Venice, water-colour; In a French Town, water-colour.

D L T OPPE COLLECTION (7)
Notes: photographs of this collection held by Mellon Centre for Studies in British Art, 20 Bloomsbury Square, WC1 071 580 0311, who have substantial Holland picture records. The collection was broken up by 1997, with the Tate Gallery acquiring much of it, including 7 or 8 Hollands. Genoa from the shore to the north, water-colour; Rouen, sketch; Ampezzo, water-colour; St.Lawrence Rouen, sketch; Cottage interior in North Wales, water-colour; Notre Dame Rouen (pair).

ROYAL HOLLOWAY COLLEGE, EGHAM (2)
Vence Piazza di San Marco, oil; Piazza di Senori Verona, oil.

RUSKIN GALLERY, STRATFORD-ON-AVON (1)
Venetian Island, water-colour. On 18 March 1964 they bought the 1831 picture The Knight's Tomb - present whereabouts unknown

SHEFFIELD, GRAVES ART GALLERY (7)
St.Honrius Cave Cintra, sketch; Lake Geneva, oil; Rialto, Rialto Venice, one oil and one water-colour; Venice, oil *; Italian Village, oil *; Salmon Trap Glen Lleddr, oil. Some pictures stored in separate Mappin Gallery. * indicates not seen during 1997 check - could not be located.

SOUTHAMPTON CITY ART GALLERY (1)
Cintra, water-colour.

STOKE CITY ART GALLERY (40)
Ilfracombe, water-colour; Paris, sketch; Flowers from Nature, oil; Venice, oil; Paris, North door of Notre Dame, oil; Venice, the Statue and the Grand Canal, oil; Venice, a Narrow Canal, oil; Venice, the Fish Market, oil; Venice, the Grand Canal, oil; River Medway - Fishing Boats off Shore, water-colour; Verona, the Ampitheatre, water-colour; Santa Maria, San Miguel, Cintra, sketch; Lilies, Paeony, Delphiniums, etc, water-colour; Tulip, Dog Rise & Love-in-a-Mist, water-colour; Knole, the Cartoon Gallery, water-colour; Paris, Rue St.George, water-colour; North Wales, the Salmon Trap, water-colour; Spanish Lady, water-colour; Naples, water-colour; Venice, across the Lagoon with the Campanile & St.Marks, water-colour; Venetian Sketch; St.Joseph Lisbon, water-colour; Trentham Hall from the Lake; Countrymen with a White Horse, oil; Anglers by a Cottage on a River Bank, oil; Windmill and boat, oil; Bunch of flowers, oil; Catching the Pig at Boston Fair, water-colour; Llangollyn, oil; Yachts, water-colour; Market Scene; Windmill; River Scene; Llyn-y-Dinas, water-colour; River Scene with Boats, water-colour and pencil; plus two more Venetian pictures, two untitled works, and a further work which could not be located at the time of a check in 1990.

TATE GALLERY (c.16)
Rouen Tour d'Horlage sketch; Rouen St.Ouen sketch; Rouen, study of arch, sketch; Rotterdam water-colour; Greenwich Hospital, oil; The Thames Below Woolwich, water-colour; Grand Canal Venice, water-colour, A Recollection of Venice, oil. In 1913 the gallery also owned View of Hyde Park Corner, oil. Additionally, in 1997 the gallery acquired the Oppe Collection, including some seven or eight Hollands, which have yet to be identified and included in this list.

TOLEDO MUSEUM OF ART (1)
Conway, oil.

VICTORIA AND ALBERT MUSEUM (45)
Alcobaco, water-colour; - Camp of the Duke of - , water-colour; Canal at Venice with Ladies, water-colour; Canal in Venice, water-colour; Carnations, water-colour; Cathedral Tower Antwerp, water-colour; Church of San Francisco Oporto, water-colour x 2; Church of SS.Giovanni E.Paolo Venice, water-colour; Cintra, water-colour x 2; Coast of Portugal Women Bathing, water-colour; Coimbra, water-colour; Doorway of Genoa Cathedral with Lion, water-colour; Entrance of the Dourdo, water-colour; Heath Scene, water-colour; James Holland the artist, by William Henry Hunt, water-colour; Hospital of the Pieta Venice, water-colour; Kensington Gardens, water-colour (not confirmed); Landscape with Buildings and Trees, water-colour; Leiria, water-colour; Manalva Palace, water-colour; Moorish Castle Mafra, water-colour; Moorish Palace Cintra, water-colour; Nymwegan, oil; Nymwegan, water-colour; Oporto, water-colour; Ospedale Civile Venice, water-colour; Os Pisoes Cintra, water-colour; Part of Old Treasury Lisbon, water-colour x 2; Porto de Moz, water-colour; The Quay, water-colour; Ramsgate near the Harbour, water-colour; The Rialto Venice, water-colour; A River Scene with Boats and Buildings, water-colour; River Scene with Windmill, water-colour (artist not confirmed); Roses, Convolvulus & Delphinium, water-colour; Roses, Poppy, Pelargonia, Delphinium & Calceolarias, water-colour; Rouen the Clock Tower, water-colour; San Francisco (Portugal), water-colour; Torre de Marca, water-colour; Torre dos Clerigos Oporto, water-colour; Torres Vedra, water-colour; Venice a SW wind after Rain, water-colour; Villa do Conde Portugal, water-colour.

WAKEFIELD ART GALLERY (1)
Courtyard in Genoa, water-colour.

WALKER ART GALLERY, LIVERPOOL (5)
Venice Capricio, water-colour; Al Marda Lisbon, water-colour; Mrs Belem's Hotel Cintra, water-colour; Port of Genoa, oil; A visit to the Shrine, oil.

WASHINGTON NATIONAL GALLERY OF ART (1)
View in North Wales, Arenig with Snowdon beyond, water-colour.

WHITWORTH GALLERY, MANCHESTER (4)
Sunset on Italian Coast, water-colour, Church of Santa Maria de la Salute Venice, water-colour, Door of the Church of St.Lawrence, Rotterdam, water-colour, Women taking their Siesta at the Unfinished Mausoleum of Don Emmanual Bathala Monastery, water-colour.

WORCESTER ART GALLERY (1)
Venice, water-colour.

APPENDIX C: WORKS EXHIBITED DURING JAMES HOLLAND'S LIFETIME

O = oil, S = sketch, W = watercolour. All British Institution works were oils

YEAR	GALLERY	TITLE & MEDIUM
1824	Royal Academy	A group of flowers W
1825	Royal Academy	Flowers W
1826	Royal Academy	Flowers W
		Study of the Belladonna Lily after nature W
1827	Royal Academy	Sketch of wild flowers, composition W
	Society of British Artists	Study of flowers after nature W
1828	Royal Academy	Flowers W
		Liscard Mill, near Liverpool W
		Flowers sketched from nature W
	Society of British Artists	Flowers W 2 works
		Flowers, wild W
		Fruit W 3 works
		Grapes W
		Hollyhocks from nature W 2 works
1829	Society of British Artists	Composition of fruit O
		Flowers W 2 works
		Fruit O 2 works
		Fruit and flowers W
		Study from nature W
	British Institution	Flowers
		Study of fruit
		Fruit W
1830	Royal Academy	Composition of flowers O
	British Institution	Study of flowers
	Society of British Artists	Fruit and flowers O
		Study of fruit O
1831	Royal Academy	College gate, Rochester
	British Institution	Greenwich Hospital
		Liscard Mill, near Liverpool
	Society of British Artists	Greenwich Hospital W
		Greenwich Pensioner O
		Greenwich Pensioner W
		Village Church W
1832	Royal Academy	Cathedral of St.Denis
	Society of British Artists	A.Brown study O
		A Study W

		Gateway O
		London from Blackheath W
		Palace of Phillipe de Bel, Paris W
		Southend bridge O
		Study from nature O 2 works
		Study from nature W
		Two sketches from nature W
1833	Royal Academy	View of London from Blackheath O
	British Institution	Front view of Greenwich Hospital
	Society of British Artists	Landscape O
		Remains of the Palace La Reine Blanche, Paris O
		View on the Ravensbourne W
		View on the Thames below Greenwich O
1834	Royal Academy	Gipsy
	British Institution	Nelson Square, Greenwich
		Scene on the Darent
		View of London from Blackheath
	Society of British Artists	A sketch of Blackwall Reach O
		Coast View W
		Evening O
		Evening W 2 works
		Hyde Park Corner and Constitution Arch O
		Sea View W
		Shipping, Bathing Machines, etc W
		Study from nature W 2 works
		Study in the Woods at Plumstead O
		Three sketches from nature W
1835	British Institution	Part of St.Mary's Chapel, Warwick
		Remains of the Palace of Phillipe La Bel, Paris
		St.Edward's Chapel, Westminster Abbey
		Society of British Artists Coast scene O
		Part of St.Edward's Chapel, Westminster Abbey, with
		the tombs of Edward III and his queen, Phillippa O
	Watercolour Society	A study from nature
		An old mill at Blackheath
		Charing Cross
		Greenwich
		On the river Tay
		The Hedge side
1836	Royal Academy	Greenwich Hospital
	British Institution	A study of flowers
	Society of British Artists	Frankfurt W
	Watercolour Society	Venice
1837	British Institution	Flowers
		Nimeguen on the Rhine
		Study from nature
		Venice
	Society of British Artists	Fishing for Minnows O
		Venice O
	Watercolour Society	Airolo Pass of the St.Gothard
		At Venice
		Landscape
		Mont Blanc from Farney (Ferney?)
		Mont Blanc from the Lake of Geneva
		St.Georgio de Grci, Venice
		Tomb of the Scaligers, Verona
		Venice - evening
1838	Royal Academy	Flowers
	British Institution	Tomb of the Scaligers, Verona
	Watercolour Society	Convent of St.Clara at the Villa de Conde, near Oporto
1839	Royal Academy	Lisbon from Port Brandas O
	British Institution	Canal Scene
		Corte della di Frari, Venice
		The Rialto, Venice
		Torres Vedras in 1838
		Venice
	Society of British Artists	Canal, Venice O
	Watercolour Society	At Lisbon
		At the Cork Convent, Cintra
		Ruins of the Monastery of Alcobaca
		The Moorish Palace, Cintra
		The Pentra Convent, Cintra
1840	British Institution	Hollyhocks
		Part of the old Fish Market, Venice
		Roses from nature
		Venice
	Society of British Artists	Milan Cathedral O

		Sketch for a picture O
		The Royal Hospital, Greenwich O
		The Tagus O
	Watercolour Society	At Lisbon
		At Venice
		Piazza Signori, Verona
1841	British Institution	St.Giorgio, Maggiori
	Society of British Artists	At Venice W
	Watercolour Society	A Trout Stream, Kent
		Chapel of St.John the Baptist in the Church of St.Rogue, Lisbon
		Flowers
		Luzern
		Milton Church, Gravesend
		On the River Ravensbourne, Kent
		Santa Cruz, Coimbra
		Venice
1842	Royal Academy	Capella del Rosario, Chiesa dei SS.Giovanni e Paulo, Venezia
		View on the Ravensbourne, Kent O
	Society of British Artists	The Return O
	Watercolour Society	Antiques
		Lisbon from Porto Brandes
		Part of the Foscari Palace
		Remainsof the Ampitheatre, Verona
		Venice
1843	British Institution	The Sailor's Home
	Society of British Artists	Canal Venice O
		Capella del Rosario dei SS.Giovanni e Paulo, Venezia O
		Chapel of the Pentra Convent, Cintra O
		Dogana da Mare Ossia di Transito, Venice O
		Flowers O
		Greenwich Pensioners O
		Italy O
		Lake of Geneva O
		On the River Colne, "The Tile House", the seat of Mortimer Drummond, Esq. in the distance O
1843	Society of British Artists	On the River Thames below Woolwich O
		Remains of the Church of St.Joseph, Lisbon W
		The Leicester Gallery, Knole House, Kent O
		The Spangled Bedroom, Knole House, Kent W
		Venice O
1844	British Institution	The Franciscan Convent, Cintra
	Society of British Artists	Devotion O
		Lake of Geneva (with Childe Harold Quotation) O
		On the Ravensbourne W
		Piazza Signori, Verona O
		The Novice W
1845	British Institution	A Gondola Race
		In the Brown Gallery, Knole
		The Bedroom of Lady Betty Germain, Knole
		The Lake of Lucerne
		The Middle Aisle of the Cathedral of Milan during the Festival of St.Carlo, Borromeo
	Society of British Artists	Chapel of St.John the Baptist, in the church of St.Rogues, Lisbon O
		Monument of Bartolommeo Colleoni (with quotation) O
		My Lady's Amanuensis O
		The Lady Betty Germain's apartments at Knole O
		The Leaning Tower of the church of St.George
		The Greek, Venice O
		Their Majesties King William IV and Queen Adelaide Visiting Greenwich Hospital, August 1835 O
1846	Royal Academy	Knole House
	British Institution	A Dutch Canal
		At Rotterdam, Status of Erasmus in the distance
		Returning from Market, Dordrecht
	Society of British Artists	A Dutch ferry boat, Amsterdam O
		London Lights after Rain, 5th November O
		Sunset O
		The Dogana, Venice O
		The Retiring of the Council of Ten W
		Venice O
1847	Royal Academy	Dover O
		Scene near the Hague, Sunset O
	British Institution	Moonlight
		On the River Maas
		Recollection of Venice, evening
		Venice

	Society of British Artists	Barbarigo Palace, Venice O
		Hastings Beach O
		Herne Bay O
		Shakespeare's Cliff O
		Summer O
		Sunset O
		Venice O
		Vespers at Maddona dell Orto O
1848	British Institution	In the Church of St.Rogue, Lisbon
		Near the Rialto, Venice
		On the Grand Canal, Venice
		The Greek Church, Venice
	Society of British Artists	Flowers O 2 works
		On the River Tagus O
		The Cathedral of Dort on the River Maas O
		The Royal Naval College, Greenwich O
		Venice - evening O
		Venice - morning O
1849	Royal Academy	Rotterdam, an October morning 2 works
	British Institution	The Chapel Room, Knole
		The Palace of La Reine Blanche
		The Rialto, Venice
1850	Royal Academy	A Morning Concert
		On the Thames below Greenwich
		Venice
	British Institution	Dover
		Piazzetta de San Marco
		Walmer Castle
1851	Royal Academy	Rouen
	British Institution	A Recollection of Venice
		Church of St.Vincent, Rouen
		Evening, after Rain
		The Colleoni Monument
1852	Royal Academy	Effect after Rain, Venice
		Tomb of the Scaligers, Verona
	British Institution	Genoa from the East Rampart, September 1851
		Lagunes de Venice
		Piazza Signori, Verona
1853	Royal Academy	S.Pier de Arena, Geneva
	British Institution	Mouth of the Bisagno, Genoa
		Part of Genoa
		Recollections of a Venetian Canal
		Salmon Trap, Glyn Lleddr
1854	Royal Academy	Rotterdam O
	British Institution	Deal Beach
		Marino Faliero, Doge of Venice
1855	British Institution	On the Grand Canal
		The Crouch Oak
		The Rialto
		Sunset
1856	British Institution	Lynmouth
		Rouen
	Watercolour Society	Market Day, Genoa
		Moonlight
		North Entrance of the Palace of Andrea Donia, Genoa
		St.Pier d'Arena, Genoese Coast
		Venetian
		Venice
1857	British Institution	Off the Lido, St.Agnes Eve
		On the Grand Canal, Venice
	Watercolour Society	Rotterdam
		St.Vincent de Rouen
		Venice
1858	British Institution	A Salmon Leap
		Fountain di S.Giorgio, Genor
		The Glen, North Wales
	Watercolour Society	D'Ampezzo
		Gesuati Chiesa, Cuvero S.Maria del Hosario
		Innsbruck
		Fountain at Innsbruck
		Venice
1859	British Institute	Basilica, S.Maree
		Inver Canoch, Inverness-shire
		St.Lawrence, Rotterdam
	Watercolour Society	Genoa - the old Mole Light
		"In Venice, Tasso's echoes are no more"
		Ponte SS.Apostoli

		Portugese Coast -Peasants Bathing
		The Cannock Burn, Inverness-shire
		The Chisholm's Pass - Col. Inge's Shooting Glen Affric, Inverness-shire
		The Post Office, Venice
		Venice
1860	British Institution	Coast of Genoa
		The House where Titian was Born
		St.Pier de Arena, Genoa
	Watercolour Society	A Fiesta, Venice
		Lisbon from Porto Brandas
		Pass D'Ampezzo, Tyrol
1861	British Institute	Arcarde, Genoa
		Brunecken, Tyrol
	Watercolour Society	Bella Venezia
1862	Watercolour Society	"Didst ever see a Gondola!"
		Roses, etc. from nature
		Rotterdam -an October morning
		The Shrine of St.Agnes
		Venezia
		Vesper time, Venice
1863	British Institution	The Lion of St.Mark
		Venezia
	Watercolour Society	A Church door - Verona
		SS.Giovanni e Paulo, Venezia - a small chapel, the ceiling decorated with pictures
		The Rialto
		Verona
		plus 35 sketches in the winter exhibition including Alcobaca & Batalha ("Recollections of an excursion to the monasteries of Alcobaca and Batalha by the author of Vathek")
1863	Watercolour Society	Below the Swallow Falls after rain, North Wales
		Church of St.Giovanni, Venice
		Convent of the Serra, Oporto and Cintra
		Di Ampezzo, Austrian Tyrol
		Off Greenwich - a recollection
		Part of the Mausoleum of Don Emanual and Interior of Pentra Convent, Cintra
		The Glen, Betws-Y-Coed
		Two sketches, Venice and Verona
		Three coloured sketches, Margate, Genoa, Clifton
		Three coloured studies - Margate, Walmer and Knole
		Three Portugese subjects
		Seven studies from nature
		Eight coloured sketches
1864	Watercolour Society	"La Cantatrice" (with quotation)
		The Dogana
		Venezia 2 works
		Venice
		Waiting for our Gondola
		plus ten frames in the winter exhibition including Cathedral, Munich, "Sketch for colour"
		Lisbon
		Lynmouth
		Mouth of the Lyn
		Santa Cruz, Coimbra, Portugal
		The Rialto
		Venice
		Venice from St.Giorgio
		Two studies
		Six sketches and studies
1865	Watercolour Society	A fruit market, Venice
		Rivalo
		Sunshine, Venice
		The Giudecca - a south wind after rain
		The Riva degli Schivoni, Venezia - a south wind
		Venezia
		plus ten frames in the winter exhibition including A Study of Light, Knole
		From nature
		Lady Betty Germain's Bedroom
		My Lady's Maids at morning. A repast at noon.
		North Wales
		On the Thames - Mill Tail
		The Cartoon Gallery, Knole
		The Venetian Bedroom, Knole

		Two studies - Inver Cannoch, Strath Glas and Glen Carrick
		Nine sketches and studies
1866	Watercolour Society	A Gleam of Sunlight
		A Highborn maiden
		Anniversary Festival of the battle of Trafalgar in the old days, when Greenwich Pensioners drank ale and smoked to celebrate great victories
		The Lion of St.Mark
		The Vesper hour
		Vico Sotto, il Campanile, Genoa
1866	Watercolour Society	12 frames in the winter exhibition including
		Batalha
		Boats, Venice
		Chapel of St.John the Baptist, Lisbon
		D'Ampezzo, Austrian Tyrol
		Genoa, from the east rampart
		Leaves from the "Dodger"
		Lyn Idwal
		Lynmouth
		Rotterdam
		Studies
		The Little Fulling Mill, N.Wales
		Two sketches in Portugal
1867	British Institution	Chapel of St.John the Baptist, Lisbon
		Greenwich Hospital as it was in 1837
		Greenwich Pensioners
		Street scene, Genoa
	Watercolour Society	The Benediction
		The St.Giorgio
		The Wind from S.W
		plus eight frames in the winter exhibition including
		Coimbra from the South, Portugal
		Light and shade
		The Kingfisher's Haunt,Lord Leigh's Park,Worcestershire
		The Lutheran Church, Rotterdam
		The River Bisagno, Genoa
		Salmon Trap, North Wales
		Sketches and studies
		Venice
1868	Watercolour Society	The Gesuati, Venice
		The Piazza Signori, Verona
		plus ten frames in the winter exhibition including
		From nature
		Gondola Race
		Rouen 2 frames
		Summer - Venice
		The Tagus
		Venice
		A page of sketches, Eastbourne
		Three sketches, two at Eastbourne and one at Margate
		Various sketches
1869	Watercolour Society	Afternoon
		Genoa, looking south east
		Genoa, near the Palazzo of Andrea di Doria
		Mid-day
		Study of Roses in my garden at Blackheath, 1839
		plus 14 frames in the winter exhibition, including
		At Ampezzo, Tyrol
		Dordt
		Milan
		Nant Mill, North Wales
		On the Cray, Kent
		The Fisherman's Song
1869	Watercolour Society	The Fish Market, Venice
		The Glen, North Wales
		The Tyrol
		Verona
		A sketch
		A study
		A study from nature
		Market Over

APPENDIX D: DATES, TOURS & EVENTS

16 Oct	1799	Born in Burslem (grave gives date as 17th).
13 Nov	1799	Elizabeth Mary Evans baptised St.Paul's Deptford, together with twin sister Hanna; daughters of William (labourer) and Mary Evans.
(c)	1801	Family moved to a farm between Burslem and Wolstanton, (Barnfield?).
25 Dec	1805	JH baptised Burslem.
	1812	Apprenticed to John Davenport, Longport Hall, Stoke. Probably lodged locally with relatives.
	1817	Charlotte Martha Morrant born.
	1819	Completed apprenticeship in the spring and left for London, but settled in Deptford. Worked in local pottery in Capperas Lane, later Bronze Street.
24 Jan	1820	(Monday). Married Elizabeth Mary Evans at St.Paul's church Deptford, by Rector William McGuire. Witnesses were Cox and Morgan.
30 Mar	1820	James Thomas born, JH described as a painter in enamels in the records. Moved to 33 Townsend St, Southwark (off Old Kent Road).
23 Apr	1820	James Thomas baptised St.Pauls's, Deptford by Rector William McGuire. Family living in Queen Street by this time.
13 May	1820	James Thomas buried St.Paul's Deptford by Rector William McGuire. JH described as a gentleman in the records.
25 Sep	1821	Elizabeth Ann Born.
17 Oct	1821	Elizabeth Ann baptised at St.George The Martyr.
By	1823	Living in Marylebone.
27 Aug	1823	Emma Lavinia born.
21 Sep	1823	Emma Lavinia baptised at St.Marylebone parish church.
	1824	Moved to 23 Warren Street, off Tottenham Court Road.
By Apr	1825	Living at 51 London St (now Maple St), Fitzroy Square.
1 Jun	1825	Thomas William born.
25 Jun	1825	Thomas William baptised at St.Pancras parish church by Rev J.Brackenbury. Father's profession given as artist. Records in GLRO under ref X30/8.
1 Jun	1827	James Henry born.
Jul/Aug	1827	May have taken family to Burslem during painting trip which included Liverpool.
16 Sep	1827	James Henry baptised at St.Pancras parish church by Rev J.Brackenbury. Father's profession artist. Records in GLRO X30/8.
12 Dec	1827	James Henry buried at St.James, Hampstead Road.
Apr	1828	Moved to 4 Queen's Row, Camberwell.
23 May	1828	Elizabeth Mary buried at St.James, Hampstead Road.
By	1829	Moved to 24 Rathbone Place, Marylebone.
	1829	Moved to 14 Rathbone Place, Marylebone.
By	1830	Moved to 51 Rathbone Place, Marylebone.
By Apr	1830	Moved to 3 Union Place, Greenwich.
	1830	Paris trip, much travelled in Kent.
Autumn	1831	Paris trip.
	1835	Trip to Scotland incl River Tay, via Warwick.
Jul-Nov	1835	Continental trip; Frankfurt, Geneva (Hotel de Europe, Oct 26-Nov 11, when left for Paris), Milan, Verona, Venice.
14 Dec	1835	Thomas William buried at St.Alfege's, Greenwich.
Dec	1835	James, son of James and Charlotte Morrant, baptised at St Mary's Lambeth
	?1836	Knole House commission.
	1836	Trips to Scotland, North Wales, Devon, East Anglia and Kent.
May-Aug	1837	Commissioned trip to Portugal.
4 Aug	1838	Timothy Edge (believed to be JH's father) died. Buried in Burslem churchyard. JH possibly attended funeral.
Autumn	1838	Trip to Portugal (including Lisbon), Spain, France and Venice.
	1838	Mary Ann Morrant housekeeping at Union Place.
	1838	Rented garden land from Morden College.
Aug	1839	Trip to Venice.
14 Feb	1840	Louisa Charlotte born in lodgings at 4 Sion Place, East St, Newington.
Autumn	1840	Trip to Venice.
	1840	Possibly living at 31 Manchester Street (evidence from banking records).
Aug	1841	Trip to Venice via Paris and Geneva. Sailed from Dover on 31 August.

	1843	Trips to Rotterdam and Venice.

1843 Trips to Rotterdam and Venice.

1844 Trip to Venice via Geneva and Verona.

Mar   1845 Moved to 11 Osnaburgh Street, Regents Park (site of present day number 32).

Aug-Oct 1845 Continental trip; Paris (22 Aug), Dordrecht, Rotterdam (23 Sep-Oct), Delft, Geneva, Verona, Venice. Left England in mid August.

12 Oct   1845 Elizabeth Ann died of smallpox at 11 Osnaburgh St.

18 Oct   1845 Elizabeth Ann buried at St.James, Hampstead Road.

Summer 1846 Trip to Portugal in late summer, stayed in Cintra hotel.

21 Jan   1847 Martha Edge (mother) died in Barnfield, Wolstanton. JH attended funeral at Burslem church.

1848 Visited Rotterdam in October and possibly Venice.

Jul-Sep 1849 Holiday with Charlotte Morrant in North Devon, including Ilfracombe and Lynmouth.

Sep   1849 Walmer.

1850 Trip to North Wales with Charlotte, including Bedgellert and Betws-Y-Coed.

Aug   1850 Trip to Rouen (20 Aug), Normandy, Paris, Geneva, Rome, Corfu and Alexandria. Returned early 1851.

By   1851 Charlotte and Louisa Charlotte living over shop at 11 South Street, Clerkenwell.

13 Apr   1851 Alice Morrant Holland born.

Sum/Aut 1851 Trip to Genoa (September) and Geneva.

1852 Trip to Paris, Genoa and Geneva, probably via Lucerne, Gotthard Pass, Lake Lucerne or Lake Maggiore, or via Frankfurt, Munich and Austria.

1853 Trip to Rotterdam and Venice.

1854 Trip to Venice.

1855 To Paris for the International Exhibition. Also to Rouen. To North Wales with Charlotte, including Snowdon (18 Sep), Nant Mill Caernarvon (26 Sep) and Conway.

Sep-   1857 Trip to Genoa, Innsbruck, D'Ampezzo in the Tyrol and Venice.

9 Oct   1857 One Henry Wrayford on the staff at Crystal Palace, writes to an unknown enquirer confirming that a picture he had presumably seen there, was painted by James Holland. Held in GLRO under ref Q/CP/13, purchased from Edward Hall of Gravesend in May 1958.and seen 6 May 94.

1858 Trip to Scotland including guest of Col Inge in Inverness-shire, Cannoc Burn, Glen Affric, Loch Benevian. Also to Venice via Innsbruck.

1859 Moved to 8 Osnaburgh Street.

1859 Trip to Portugal, Spain, Southern France, Genoa and Venice.

16 Jul   1860 Emma Lavinia died. Buried at Highgate.

Autumn 1860 Trip to Venice.

1861 Daughters returned to Osnaburgh St, but not Charlotte, who took them away again to 10 Orchard Street, Camden Town.

1861 Emily West moved in.

Early   1862 Dropped association with Emily West, who moved to 15 Grafton Street, Fitzroy Square.

1862 Trip to Venice.

30 May 1863 Louisa marries Arthur Hird at St.Pancras church.

Summer 1863 Visited Burslem and Keele Hall.

26 Jan   1864 Mary Ann Morrant died at Osnaburgh St. Buried Highgate.

10 Feb   1864 William Henry Hunt ("Old Billy") died. Buried Highgate.

1864 Drew up his will at 23 Guildford St, Russell Square.

10 May 1864 Amy Louisa Hird (1st grandchild) born.

1864 Sarah Ellis Morrant became housekeeper. Charlotte probably returned.

Autumn 1864 Trip to Venice.

1865 Trip to Venice.

22 Sep   1865 James Henry Arthur Hird born.

Jan   1866 James Henry Arthur baptised St.Pancras parish church.

5 Nov   1866 Frederick Charles Hird born.

3 Feb   1870 (Wednesday) Isabella Alice Hird born.

12 Feb   1870 James Holland died of cirrhosis of the liver at 8 Osnaburgh Street. Buried at Highgate.

1870 Charlotte, Alice and Sarah moved to Stewarts Grove, Tottenham.

12 Aug 1909 Charlotte Morrant died. Buried Forest Hill.

APPENDIX E: SELECTED BIBLIOGRAPHY

ART JOURNAL - Carried an obituary.

ATHENAEUM CLUB. - Published an obituary notice; "In later years, contributed to the management of the Old Watercolour Society, with John Gilbert and Frederick Burton (both afterwards knighted), he formed the special committee appointed to arrange the winter exhibition of sketches. They say he "was famous for anecdote."

CATALOGUE OF THE COLLECTION OF FREDERICK JOHN NETTLEFOLD, 1925. Grundy.
Vol II P.196 lists Holland painting(s).

DICTIONARY OF ARTISTS, McGraw-Hill.

JAMES HOLLAND - DIRECT QUOTES. - On April 24 1837 he wrote to a patron (Mr Edward Magrath, Secretary of the Athenaeum Club), "pray believe me when I assure you it is more a want of confidence in my own powers that has hitherto kept me from sending to the Royal Academy, than to any want of faith in their disposition to do justice to any talented artist. I will henceforth devote myself to painting, and look forward with hope to something worthy notice." He also said, "Parting with a sketch, was like parting with a tooth. Once sold it cannot be replaced."

JENNINGS LANDSCAPE ANNUAL (1839), Robert Jennings, 62 Cheapside.
Holland commissioned to do a series of drawings for annual entitled "The Tourist in Portugal", text by W.H.Harrison. 18 pictures appeared in the book.

MODERN PAINTERS (1843), Ruskin. - Section V "Of Truth of Water" Chap II; "I have seen, some seven years ago, works by J.Holland which were I think, as near perfection as watercolour can be carried - for bona fide truth, refined and finished to the highest degree."

OLD WATERCOLOUR SOCIETY, BANKSIDE GALLERY, 48, HOPTON STREET, BLACKFRIARS, SE1 9JH. - OWSC Journal 1930 (Vol VII); Mentions apprenticeship at Davenports at age 12 and the obituaries in the Times 16.2.70 and Illustrated London News 19.2.70. OWSC Journal 1966 (Vol XLII); Holland took a flower painting and one of a linnet to Davenport and was employed at once to Davenport and was employed at once. "Served his time as an honourary member of the Society of British Artists."

OXFORD HISTORY OF ENGLISH ART VOLUME 10.

ROGET'S HISTORY OF THE OLD WATERCOLOUR SOCIETY.

STAFFORDSHIRE MAGAZINE. - The June 1973 edition, carries an article about Holland by Morley Tonkin.

STOKE-ON-TRENT MUSEUM ARCHAEOLOGICAL SOCIETY, J.H.Kelly, 1969.
Report No.3, 1968, features excavations on the site of the former Holland pottery works at Hill Top, Burslem.

STOKES, HUGH. "JAMES HOLLAND 1800-1870". London 1927, included in Walkers Quarterly Volume XXIII.

WALKER'S QUARTERLY. - Volume XXIII published "James Holland, 1800-1870" by Hugh Stokes.

Flower Study
Watercolour, 1823. The Potteries Museum and Art Gallery, Stoke on Trent.

Cathedral Tower, Antwerp
Watercolour. Victoria and Albert Museum.

Heath Scene
Watercolour. Victoria and Albert Museum.

River Scene with Windmill
Watercolour. Victoria and Albert Museum.

Llyn-Y-Dinas. North Wales
Watercolour.
The Potteries Museum and Art Gallery,
Stoke on Trent.

A Canal in Venice
Watercolour.
Victoria and Albert Museum.

Rouen Clock Tower
Sketch, August 1850.
Victoria and Albert Museum.

Nymegen, Holland
Watercolour.
Victoria and Albert Museum.

Villa do Conde, Portugal. Watercolour, September, 1837. Victoria and Albert Museum.

Ospedale Civile, Venice
Watercolour, 1858. Victoria and Albert Museum.

Convento da Serra, Portugal
Watercolour, September 1837. Victoria and Albert Museum.

Roses, Poppy, Pelargonia, Delphinium
and Calceolarias
Watercolour, 1859.
Victoria and Albert Museum.

River Scene with Boats
Watercolour.
The Potteries Museum and Art Gallery,
Stoke on Trent.

Anglers by a Cottage on a River Bank
Oil. The Potteries Museum and Art Gallery, Stoke on Trent.

Countrymen with a White Horse.
Oil. The Potteries Museum and Art Gallery, Stoke on Trent.

Santa Maria, San Miguel, Cintra
Sketch, 1837. The Potteries Museum and Art Gallery, Stoke on Trent.

Venice
Watercolour, 1856. The Potteries Museum and Art Gallery, Stoke on Trent.

Hospital of the Pieta, Venice
Watercolour, 1844. Victoria and Albert Museum.

Landscape with Buildings and Trees
Watercolour. Victoria and Albert Museum.

St Joseph's, Lisbon
Watercolour, 1837.
The Potteries Museum and Art Gallery,
Stoke on Trent.
Annotated by the artist - "Destroyed by the
earthquake".

Doorway of Genoa Cathedral, with Lion
Watercolour, 1851.
Victoria and Albert Museum.

Ramsgate, near the Harbour
Watercolour. Victoria and Albert Museum.

Venice, a South-West Wind after Rain
Watercolour, 1864. Victoria and Albert Museum.

Venice
Oil, 1851. The Potteries Museum and Art Gallery, Stoke on Trent.